EDITOR-IN-CHIEF: Caty Bérubé

EDITORIAL PRODUCTION TEAM LEADER: Crystel Jobin-Gagnon

GRAPHIC PRODUCTION TEAM LEADER: Marie-Christine Langlois

PRODUCTION COORDINATOR: Marjorie Lajoie

CONTENT MANAGER: Catherine Pelletier

AUTHORS: Benoit Boudreau, Éric Dacier and Richard Houde.

CHEFS: Benoit Boudreau, Éric Dacier and Richard Houde.

WRITERS: Miléna Babin, Stéphanie Boisvert, Fernanda Machado Gonçalves
and Raphaële St-Laurent Pelletier.

COPY EDITORS: Edmonde Barry, Marilou Cloutier, Corinne Dallain and Viviane St-Arnaud.

PRODUCTION ASSISTANT: Nancy Morel

GRAPHIC DESIGNERS: Sonia Barbeau, Sheila Basque, Annie Gauthier, Marie-Chloë G. Barrette
and Karyne Ouellet.

FOOD STYLING SUPERVISOR: Christine Morin

FOOD STYLISTS: Laurie Collin, Maude Gagnon, Maude Grimard and Lauréanne Hallé.

PHOTO SUPERVISOR: Marie-Ève Lévesque

PHOTOGRAPHERS: Mélanie Blais, Jean-Christophe Blanchet and Rémy Germain.

PHOTOGRAPHERS AND VIDEOGRAPHERS: Tony Davidson and Francis Gauthier.

IMAGE PROCESSING AND CALIBRATION SPECIALIST: Yves Vaillancourt

COLLABORATORS: Julie Day-Lebel and Nicholas Giguère.

TRANSLATION: Edgar

Bibliothèque et Archives nationales du Québec and Library and Archives Canada cataloguing in publication

Title: 5 ingredients, 15 minutes : the 125 best recipes for quick and easy dinners / Benoit Boudreau,
Richard Houde, Éric Dacier.

Other titles: 5 ingrédients, 15 minutes. English | Five ingredients, fifteen minutes

Names: Boudreau, Benoit, - author. | Houde, Richard, - author. | Dacier, Éric, 1977- author.

Description: Series statement: Livre 5-15 | Translation of: 5 ingrédients, 15 minutes. |
Includes bibliographical references and an index.

Identifiers: Canadiana 20190025565 | ISBN 9782896588169

Subjects: LCSH: Quick and easy cooking. | LCGFT: Cookbooks.

Classification: LCC TX833.5 B6813 2019 | DDC 641.5/55—dc23

Director of distribution: Marcel Bernatchez

Distribution: Éditions Pratico-Pratiques inc. and Messageries ADP.

Printing: TC Interglobe

Legal deposit: 3rd quarter 2019
Bibliothèque et Archives nationales du Québec
Library and Archives Canada
ISBN 978-2-89658-816-9

Gouvernement du Québec. Refundable Tax Credit for Book Publishing program – Gestion SODEC

7710 Wilfrid-Hamel Boulevard, Québec, QC G2G 2J5
Tel.: 418-877-0259
Toll-free: 1-866-882-0091
Fax: 418-780-1716
www.pratico-pratiques.com

Comments and suggestions: info@pratico-pratiques.com

5 ingredients 15 minutes

THE 125 BEST RECIPES
for quick and easy dinners

Table of contents

125 incredible recipes for perfect quick dinners

Our *5-15* cookbooks are based on a very simple idea: to gather a wide selection of quick recipes that can be made in 15 minutes, tops, and with only 5 ingredients. Since we started this adventure, the most important goal for us has been to help families and busy people save time in the kitchen and to encourage healthy eating habits. With a focus on simplicity and speed without compromising taste, *5-15* recipes are also great for those who don't know how to cook or are inexperienced in the kitchen.

In this book, we offer over a hundred recipes that can be made with 5 ingredients in 15 minutes, all based on a single guiding principle: to enjoy a maximum of flavours using as few products—and as little time—as possible! You'll discover the best recipes to help you win the race against the clock come dinner time, along with plenty of tips and advice to help you stay organized and efficient as you cook up meals everyone will love.

Soups, sautés, salads, casseroles, pasta, pizzas, burgers... We've included everything you need to make your busy evening menus more delicious than ever, whether you love meat, fish or vegetarian dishes.

Hope you're hungry!

The 5-15 team

The ABCs of quick and easy cooking

Can you really make delicious meals even when you've got no time to spare? Why, of course! Just follow these surefire tips and use clever shortcuts like precut vegetables, seasoning blends and precooked pasta. No more need to fall back on ready-to-eat meals or dashing out to the nearest takeout. We're revealing all our secrets to help you make home cooking as efficient as possible!

Whether you're trying to save money, don't have the time or just don't feel like spending hours in the kitchen, the idea of nutritious meals ready in just a few minutes is appealing to pretty much everyone! But how to find the happy middle ground between healthy eating and quick cooking? With home-assembled meals! Home-assembled meals are just what they sound like, a mix of a prepared, semi-prepared and fresh ingredients. This technique lets you cook balanced meals while making the most of your time and money, and is key to the "5 ingredients – 15 minutes" concept. With home assembly, you can make dishes in a flash by replacing long ingredient lists with all kinds of ingenious shortcuts in order to serve up food in record time. These tasty, nutritious meals are certain to please both young and old!

Home-assembled meals are such a success because they combine store-bought products with nutritious fresh ingredients for meals that are as fast as they are balanced. For example, prepared items, like whole cooked chicken, pasta sauces or pesto, and semi-prepared items, like frozen vegetable blends, precooked rice or shredded cheese, are excellent starting points for quick dinners. When combined with fresh vegetables, meat or legumes, these lifesaving ingredients are easily turned into healthy meals that are ready in a jiffy. Proof that the fastest option isn't always your neighbourhood takeout!

Quick and easy cooking involves shortcuts, but it's also a matter of organization, resourcefulness and sometimes even a dash of creativity! To make it easier for you to prepare dinner, we've assembled our top tips (tried and true!) for simplifying your daily life, from organizing your pantry to planning a weekly menu. Eating well every day is a lot less complicated than you might think!

Organisation 101

Never underestimate how important proper organization is to meal prep! It's the key not just to success in the kitchen, but to enjoying yourself as well!

The grocery list

To prevent food waste and save money, take a look at what you've got in your pantry, fridge and freezer before making a grocery list. If you usually shop at the same place every week, try grouping the ingredients on your list by section of the grocery store to save you having to traipse up and down the same aisles. Finally, try asking the kids for help putting away groceries. They could even help peel fruits and vegetables, shred cheese or portion out individual servings of snacks!

BELL PEPPER BEEF
Prep time: 15 minutes • Cook time on low: 6 hours • Serves: 4

PER PORTION	
Calories	658
Protein	36 g
Fat	37 g
Carbohydrates	47 g
Fibre	1 g
Iron	6 mg
Calcium	110 mg
Sodium	538 mg

Diced tomatoes drained
1 can (540 ml)

Steak spice
15 ml (1 tbsp)

Demi-glace sauce
or beef gravy 125 ml
(½ cup)

Beef cubes for stew
720 g (about 1 2/3 lb)

Bell peppers 1 green
and 1 red cut into cubes

1 onion chopped

Cornstarch 15 ml (1 tbsp)

Worcestershire sauce
30 ml (2 tbsp)

1. Place the diced tomatoes, steak spice, demi-glace sauce, onion, and Worcestershire sauce, if desired, in a large freezer bag. Close the bag and shake to mix.

2. Add the beef cubes to the bag and shake until the meat is fully coated with the sauce. Remove the air from the bag and seal it.

3. Place the bell peppers in another large freezer bag. Remove the air from the bag and seal it.

4. The night before your meal, let the bags thaw out in the refrigerator.

5. When ready to cook, transfer the beef preparation to the slow cooker. Cover and cook on low for 5 hours and 30 minutes to 6 hours and 30 minutes.

6. Drain the thawed bell peppers and add them to the slow cooker. Dissolve the cornstarch in a little cold water. Add to the slow cooker and stir.

Recipe prep

Before starting a recipe, always take the time to read it in full and get out all of the ingredients and tools you will need. Chop all your vegetables in advance and measure out the ingredients. That way, you can concentrate on cooking and avoid careless mistakes.

A bolt of inspiration

How often does this happen to you? You're just about to head out to the grocery store when you realize you're all out of ideas for dinner. To avoid spinning your wheels thinking of what to make, keep a list of quick and easy recipes pinned to the fridge. Pick meals the whole family likes, and you'll always have inspiration right in front of you when you're making your grocery list. Separate the recipes by category so that you have a balanced menu every week (pasta, stew, beef, vegetarian, fish, etc.). Encourage your family members to add any new recipes they discover. You'll never be short on ideas again!

Practical tools

The right tools can save you so much time in the kitchen! With a mandolin, you can julienne and finely slice carrots, cucumbers, beets and zucchini, while a garlic press minces fresh garlic in no time flat! Also think about getting yourself a good-quality zester and cheese grater so you can safely zest and grate ingredients with ease!

1 ingredient
=
2 recipes

When shopping for groceries, consider ingredients that can be used for multiple recipes. For example, a white sauce like bechamel can be used for pasta one night and for vol-au-vent the next day, a roast chicken can be used to make hot chicken as well as fried rice, and spaghetti sauce can be used for sloppy joes!

Long live leftovers

It may not be the most exciting thing to make dinner out of the odds and ends in your pantry, fridge and freezer, but it can be just as tasty, and useful to boot! By making one or two meals a week out of your leftover ingredients, you're treating yourself to a well-deserved break from meal prep, saving money on your grocery bill and preventing food waste. It's the perfect opportunity to empty the contents of your saucepans and eat those lonely vegetables in the back of the crisper! Viva leftovers!

Tidy cupboards

If your cupboards, pantry or drawers are disorganized, it can take ages to find the right kitchen tool or ingredient. To get your kitchen running on all cylinders, make an effort to keep your cupboards in order and try storing items you use frequently within arm's reach.

Get a head start with Sunday cooking

Weekday meal prep gets quicker and easier when you develop these habits for the weekend! Get inspired by these practical tips and you'll be breathing easier when it's time to cook dinner!

Prepare your produce

When you get home from the grocery store, ask your family members to help you wash and prepare fruits and vegetables for snacks and meals. For example, carrots and celery can be washed and cut into sticks, lettuce can be washed, dried, wrapped in paper towel and placed in a plastic bag in the fridge, broccoli and cauliflower can be washed and chopped into small florets, and watermelon can be sliced or cut into cubes and put away in airtight containers. And those are just a few ideas!

Shredded cheese

Although you can always buy pre-shredded cheese, bricks of cheese are cheaper. To save time, shred your cheese when you get back from the grocery store, then place it all in an airtight bag in the fridge. That way, you can quickly access shredded cheese whenever you need it and eliminate the drudgery of extra dishes!

Ready-to-use protein

Some protein (chicken, pork, tofu, beef) can be trimmed or sliced up in advance, then frozen or refrigerated. This trick will save you having to wash an extra cutting board and knife every time you cook. You'll then be ready to season and cook your protein when you need it. You can even add the marinade at this step in some cases.

Hard-boiled eggs to the rescue

Hard-boiled eggs in their shell will keep in the fridge for a week. Make a habit of cooking some on Sunday: you'll have something to put on your toast for mornings when you've got no time to spare, or for adding to a makeshift sandwich, salad or soup. It's a practical tip that helps you eat well without having to think too hard about it!

Freezer bags

Are you familiar with the freezer bag method? You simply prep your recipe ingredients in advance (washing, cutting, marinating, etc.) and place them in a single freezer bag. This is particularly useful for recipes where everything's cooked together at once (sheet pan meals, stews, stir-fries, etc.). When you're ready, defrost the contents of the bag, dump everything in the pan or slow cooker or onto the sheet pan, and presto!

Precooked starches and grains

If it's Sunday and you're planning on eating rice, pasta or quinoa during the upcoming week, why not cook it in advance and keep it in the fridge in an airtight container? That way, all you have to do is reheat it in the microwave when you need it, or just toss it straight into cold salads!

Double your recipes

Doubling a recipe takes less energy and dirties fewer dishes than making two separate meals! The next time you're planning to make a pot pie, lasagna, spaghetti sauce or anything else that freezes well, get enough ingredients to double (or even triple) the recipe and freeze a portion. Then, you'll have a premade meal as backup for the following weeks!

Ready-to-go marinades

Marinades are unparalleled when it comes to infusing dishes with flavour, but they can really lengthen the time it takes to make a meal. So why not make them in advance? Got a master marinade? Double or triple your recipe and freeze it in ice trays or leave it in the fridge for up to 48 hours. You can also make a big batch of dry rub for speedy pork roasts and chicken thighs!

10 lifesaving ingredients for dinner in a hurry

Keeping certain ingredients in your pantry, fridge or freezer at all times can help you eat healthy every night, even when you're pressed for time. Here are some ideas for ingredients to keep on hand for improvised, super-fast dinners!

1. Canned fish

Canned tuna and salmon are cheap and nutritious sources of protein that can be used to whip up meals in no time. Add them to soups, sandwiches, salads and pasta, or mix them with cream cheese to enhance a meal with a protein-packed spread. And why not mix things up with flavoured versions?

Since these ingredients keep well, stock up whenever they're on sale!

2. Rice

The different varieties of rice (basmati, brown, wild, etc.) are super versatile and a great way to use up lots of leftover ingredients in the fridge. Do so with a delicious fried rice—all it takes is cooked rice, leftover meat (chicken, pork roast, ham, etc.) cut into small pieces, some chopped vegetables (onions, carrots, celery, etc.) and an egg!

3. Pasta

Dry pasta is super handy when you need to make dinner with just the ingredients you've got on hand, like leftover meat, cold cuts, cheese or vegetables. Though pasta goes great with lots of sauce, it's also tasty with just a knob of butter or a drizzle of olive oil.

4. Eggs

There are a million ways to add eggs to your meals! Don't limit yourself to just the traditional egg salads, quiches and omelettes—there are so many other quick recipes that benefit from eggs. How about a hard-boiled egg (halved) in a bowl of soup, a sunny-side egg as a pizza topping, or a soft-boiled egg in a salad?

5. Frozen veggies

We'd be crazy to ignore frozen vegetables, given that they've got just as many vitamins as fresh ones! So stock up on edamame, spinach, corn, peas and spaghetti sauce blends. That way, you'll always have vegetables ready to go for stir-fries, soups, casseroles or pasta!

6. Firm tofu

Tofu takes great to freezing—it even absorbs marinades better if it's frozen and defrosted first! You can cut strips or blocks of firm tofu when you get back from the grocery store and stick them in an airtight bag in the freezer. Once you're ready, place the bag in a bowl of lukewarm water to defrost the tofu, then press it to squeeze out the excess water. Finally, marinate it for 20 minutes before cooking.

7. Legumes

We love canned legumes! You can add them to couscous salads, quinoa, rice, and even soups! Beans can be used to make chili or speedy nachos, while chickpeas are perfect for vegetarian curries and homemade hummus!

8. Nuts and seeds

There are so many different kinds of nuts and seeds out there (almonds, peanuts, cashews, walnuts, pumpkin seeds, sunflower seeds, etc.), which is great because they're the perfect way to pack protein into snacks and weekday meals! You can add them to cereals and granola bars, or toss them into stir-fries, green salads, pasta salads and soups!

9. Canned tomatoes

You should always have diced tomatoes, tomato sauce or to-mato paste in your pantry. They can be used to make all kinds of easy and tasty recipes, including pizzas, stews, cheesy pasta, chicken or eggplant Parmesan, and soups. Make sure to stock up on these handy ingredients to help you out in a pinch!

10. Frozen smoked salmon

Smoked salmon has the benefit of defrost-ing in record time and adds a festive touch to weekday meals. It can be eaten hot or cold and goes great in paninis, omelettes, pastas and gratins, as well as atop pizzas or salads. It's also very convenient to have in the freezer if guests drop in unannounced! If you buy a whole smoked salmon, divide it into portions before freezing, as it can't be put back in the freezer once it defrosts.

The biggest flavour-boosting ingredients

Do your recipes sometimes lack punch? Honestly, you wouldn't believe how easy it is to add that special "wow" factor to your dishes! Certain ingredients, even in small doses, are blessed with the ability to enhance flavours and excite the taste buds. Here's our favourite ingredients that will make your meals burst with flavour every time!

◆ **Fresh herbs**

Dill

Dill has a delicate, fresh flavour that goes incredibly with fish and seafood recipes, such as seafood sauces, tartare, fish cakes and smoked salmon bagels. But it's also delicious as a garnish on soups, as well as in pasta or potato salads!

Chives

Chives have a very strong flavour that is similar to green onion, which it can be substituted for in any recipe: green salads, pasta or potato salads, gratins, warm dips, quiches, omelettes, flavoured butter, stuffed potatoes, devilled eggs, foil-packet fish or veggies, etc.

Cilantro

Cilantro steals the show in many Mexican-inspired recipes, like guacamole, tacos and fajitas, but it also dazzles in Asian dishes, like Thai or Vietnamese soups, stir-fries and spring rolls. Its unique, fresh taste also goes great with salads and soups of any kind.

Basil

Basil is the best friend of tomato-based dishes, such as tomato macaroni au gratin, Margherita pizza, spaghetti sauce, tomato soup, tomato gazpacho or Caprese skewers. You can also add it to fruity desserts and snacks, such as smoothies, strawberry mousse and fruit salads.

Mint

Mint is often used in chocolate-based desserts, but it's also tasty in smoothies, fruit salads and mousses. It adds a blast of freshness to summery salads, green soups (pea, spinach, leek, etc.) and Vietnamese dishes (spring rolls, pho, etc.).

Parsley

Parsley has subtle flavours that are perfect for pairing with traditional French cuisine. Finely chopped, it can be added to flavoured butter, soups, stews, foil-packet white fish or veggies, as well as to homemade mayonnaise and dressings. It also tastes great in pasta salads and couscous salads.

Rosemary

Rosemary has a piney, strongly aromatic flavour. You can add whole sprigs of it to flavour potato casseroles or beef or pork stews. You can also finely chop rosemary needles to add to marinades, butter or homemade mayo.

◆ Spices

Salt-free seasoning blend

Salt-free seasoning is a blend of dried spices meant to kick up the flavour of your food without raising the dish's sodium content. This salt substitute is useful for poultry, pork, fish, soups and crudités (tomato, cucumber, etc.). You can find it at the grocery store or make it at home. In a salt shaker, just mix equal parts of your favourite dried spices: garlic or onion powder, celery seed, mustard powder, paprika, thyme, pepper, etc.

Turmeric

Turmeric comes from the rhizome (underground stem) of a plant from South Asia. It can be purchased either raw, or as a dry, ground spice. It has a peppery, earthy and lightly spicy flavour. Add turmeric to Indian dishes like butter chicken and curries, as well as to legume-based salads and recipes with scrambled eggs. You can also use it to spice up mayonnaise, dips and marinades.

Ginger

Ginger can be purchased in two different forms: fresh or as a dried powder. It has a very strong flavour, fragrant and spicy, that's perfect in its namesake gingerbread, and in countless cookies and desserts. It's extremely versatile, and is as delicious in stir-fries and Asian soups as in marinades and Indian curries.

Nutmeg

Nutmeg is the fruit of an evergreen tree from Indonesia. You can find it either as a powder or as a seed that must be finely grated. It adds a fragrant touch to desserts and snacks (cookies, granola bars, cakes and breads), and to savoury dishes too. It brilliantly flavours bechamel sauce for gratins, lasagnas and vol-au-vent, and can also be used in omelettes and soups.

Smoked paprika

Smoked paprika is a powdered spice made from a type of mild red pepper. Its naturally smoky taste gives an edge to myriad recipes, including veggie casserole, chicken, pork roast, spaghetti sauce and grilled shrimp. It can also give a boost to homemade mayo served with burgers and fries.

Garlic powder or onion powder

Garlic and onion powder are two spices you can't do without if you want to enhance the flavour of your meals without dirtying extra dishes and making life more complicated. A pinch is enough to punch up white sauces, gravy, mayonnaise, vinaigrettes, soups, omelettes, devilled eggs, stews and other dishes.

◆ Condiments and more

Maple syrup

Maple syrup is one ingredient you should always have handy when cooking. It's great not just for desserts, but for a wide variety of recipes. Its unique and rich taste is scrumptious in marinades (pork, poultry, beef, fish, lamb, duck), roasted vegetable casseroles (Brussels sprouts, potatoes, beets, etc.), sauces, vinaigrettes, mayonnaise and dips.

Dijon mustard

The sharp taste of Dijon mustard with its hint of vinegar adds flair to any sandwich or sub, but can also quickly jazz up a tasty mac and cheese, pork chop, chicken cordon bleu, glazed salmon or melted Brie! Not to mention the kick it gives homemade vinaigrettes, sauces and mayo.

Citrus juice and zest

The juice and zest of lemons, limes and oranges is useful for cooking superb dishes even when you've only got a few ingredients on hand. The juice adds a rather acidic note, while the zest is only mildly bitter and very aromatic, which is great for pastas, salads, tartare, sauces, vinaigrettes and desserts.

Hot sauce

Whether or not you're a hot sauce lover, it's good to know that you can use hot sauces like Sriracha, sambal oelek and Tabasco in small amounts to enhance the flavour of your dishes without cranking up the heat. Just add a few drops to your vinaigrettes, marinades and mayo, and you'll really notice the difference!

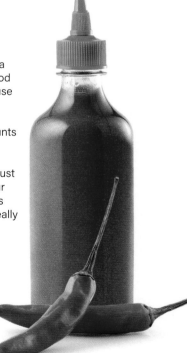

Liquid smoke

Liquid smoke, available in your average supermarket, allows you to infuse your protein with fantastic barbecue flavour. However, it loses its intensity as it cooks, so just add a little bit at the last minute to shrimp, chicken breasts and wings, burgers, or crispy tofu.

Flavoured butter

Flavoured butter is perfect for jazzing up steaks, fillets of salmon or other fish, and corn on the cob. Just mix spices, fresh herbs and citrus zest into softened butter, then use plastic wrap to roll it into a log shape. Let the butter set in the fridge, then slice yourself a pat whenever you need it!

White and red wine

If you've got a few glugs of red or white wine left in the bottle after dinner, try freezing some in an ice cube tray, so that you've always got it on hand for cooking. Wine can be used to deglaze plans when making sauces, stocks, warm dips and braised meat. Just a touch is enough to class up your week-day meals!

Sour cream

When added right before serving, sour cream gives a creamy texture to any number of dishes, as well as balancing out the acidity of tomato-based recipes. This is the case for smoked salmon or vegetable pizzas, stuffed potatoes, stews, curries, butter chicken, nachos and vibrant soups.

Pesto

Whether homemade or store-bought, pesto is one of those all-purpose foods that can liven up any kind of dish. Add it to soups, quiches, omelettes and all sorts of pasta, spread it on chicken breasts or salmon fillets before baking, or use it as a substitute for tomato sauce with your pizzas and pastas!

Soy sauce

Soy sauce is super salty and can really amp up the flavour of your protein (salmon fillets, tofu strips, chicken thighs, etc.), especially in Asian-inspired recipes. You can also use it to enhance veggie fried rice, soups, mayo, dips and vinaigrettes.

Fish sauce

Fish sauce is often served with imperial rolls, spring rolls and dumplings. You can also use it to punch up vinaigrettes and marinades for pork, chicken and fish. Its flavour diminishes while cooking, so add it right at the end for the most impact.

Hoisin sauce

Hoisin sauce is thick, with a sweet and mildly acidic flavour. You can use it to glaze chicken and duck, caramelize pork tenderloin or jazz up fried rice and soups. You can also add it to marinades. Careful: hoisin sauce has a tendency to burn if it's cooked in a pan on high heat with other ingredients.

Sesame oil

Sesame oil comes in both toasted and untoasted varieties, with the former having a stronger flavour. Its pronounced sesame taste can flavour Asian soups, fried rice and peanut-based stews. It can also be used to season mayo, marinades and homemade vinaigrettes.

Substitute ingredients like a chef

Here are a few ideas for substituting basic ingredients in your recipes when you don't have what you need at home!

Fresh herbs

If a recipe calls for fresh herbs and you don't have any on hand, you can always swap them for dried herbs. That said, dried herbs are denser and sometimes have a stronger flavour, which means that if you want your dishes to turn out the same, you'll need to convert your measurements based on the following formula:

15 ml (1 tbsp) chopped
fresh herbs
=
5 ml (1 tsp)
dried herbs

Garlic cloves

Need fresh garlic but don't have any at home? Consider swapping it for garlic powder. It's much more concentrated than fresh garlic, so you only need to use about an eighth as much:

1 garlic clove = 0.5 to 1.25 ml
(⅛ tsp to ¼ tsp) garlic powder

Cheese

In general, you can substitute any cheese with another of the same firmness. For example, mozzarella, a firm cheese, can be replaced by many other cheeses such as Cheddar, Gouda, Oka, Gruyère and Emmenthal. Cream cheese, a spreadable cheese, can be swapped for fresh goat cheese, Boursin or ricotta. And any soft cheese, such as Brie, can be replaced with another soft one such as Camembert. However, even though bocconcini is also a soft cheese, it should be substituted with fresh mozzarella.

Pasta

Since all the different varieties of wheat-based pasta are basically made from the same ingredients, you can always replace one with another, so long as you choose pastas of the same length. You might also want to consider veggie spirals, which can replace spaghetti in many recipes!

- **Spaghetti:** spaghettini, angel hair, linguine
- **Penne:** tortiglioni, rigatoni
- **Macaroni:** farfalle, fusilli, gemelli
- **Orzo:** conchigliette (small shells), orecchiette

White fish

Though the different types of white fish might taste similar enough, they have a wide variety of textures. To make your meal a success, make sure to substitute one white fish for another of the same kind.

- **Delicate:** basa, ocean perch
- **Semi-firm:** bass, cod, haddock, sole, turbot
- **Firm:** tilapia, mahi-mahi, halibut

Frozen vegetables

If a recipe calls for a frozen veggie blend, you can always replace it with fresh vegetables. A good rule of thumb is to try to cut all the veggies the same size so they cook evenly! Here's an estimate of how many vegetables are needed for each blend, using similar proportions of each vegetable. Go ahead and adapt them to your taste, needs and what you have on hand.

Vegetables for soup (750 g)

Vegetable	Cut	Suggested amount		
Green beans	Medium-sized pieces	Approximately 10 to 12 green beans	OR	Approximately 250 ml (1 cup) of each vegetable
Rutabaga	Diced	Approximately ½ a small rutabaga		
Onion	Diced	Approximately 1½ onions		
Celery	Diced	Approximately 2 celery stalks		
Carrot	Diced	Approximately 1½ carrots		

Mixed vegetables (750 g)

Vegetable	Cut	Suggested amount		
Green beans	Medium-sized pieces	Approximately 20 to 24 green beans	OR	Approximately 500 ml (2 cups) of each vegetable
Green peas	Whole	2 cans (284 ml each)		
Corn kernels	Whole	2 cans (199 ml each)		

Diced vegetable mix (750 g)

Vegetable	Cut	Suggested amount		
Onion	Diced	Approximately 1½ onions	OR	Approximately 250 ml (1 cup) of each vegetable
Celery	Diced	Approximately 3 stalks of celery		
Carrot	Diced	Approximately 1½ carrots		
Green pepper	Diced	Approximately 1½ peppers		
Red pepper	Diced	Approximately 1½ peppers		

California blend (750 g)

Vegetable	Cut	Suggested amount		
Broccoli	Small florets	Approximately 1 head of broccoli	OR	Approximately 500 ml (2 cups) of each vegetable
Cauliflower	Small florets	Approximately ½ a cauliflower		
Carrot	Rounds	Approximately 3 carrots		

Stir-fry vegetable mix (750 g)

Vegetable	Cut	Suggested amount (if choosing 5 vegetables)		
Green beans	Whole	Approximately 10 to 12 green beans	OR	Approximately 250 ml (1 cup) of each vegetable
Carrot	In sticks	Approximately 1½ carrots		
Broccoli	In small florets	Approximately ½ a head of broccoli		
Snow peas	Whole	Approximately 10 to 12 snow peas		
Onion	Diced	Approximately 1½ onions		
Red pepper	In strips	Approximately 1½ peppers		
Water chestnuts	Sliced	1 can (227 ml)		
Mushrooms	Sliced	Approximately 7 to 8 mushrooms		
Baby corn	Whole	Approximately 5 to 6 baby corns		

The vegetables in different blends for Asian stir-fries vary greatly depending in the type of blend and brand. To make your own mix, just choose five vegetables from the list.

CHICKEN

If you love chicken, this section will have your mouth watering in no time! Discover Indian, Asian, Mexican and Italian flavours alongside the classics you know and love. All you have to do is decide which of these simple and delicious recipes you'll be serving up tonight!

1 **Garlic butter**
80 ml (⅓ cup)

2 **Chicken**
4 skinless breasts,
cubed

3 **Frozen mixed vegetables**
500 ml (2 cups)

4 **Condensed cream of chicken soup**
store-bought
2 cans (284 ml each)

5 **Flaky roll dough**
like Pillsbury
brand
1 can (340 g)

ALSO NEEDED:
● **1 onion**
chopped

Skillet Chicken Pot Pie

Prep time **15 minutes** • Cook time **24 minutes** • Serves **4**

PER SERVING	
Calories	815
Protein	46 g
Fat	41 g
Carbohydrates	66 g
Fibre	7 g
Iron	4 mg
Calcium	90 mg
Sodium	2,178 mg

Preparation

1. Preheat the oven to 205°C (400°F).

2. Melt half the butter in an ovenproof skillet over medium heat. Cook the chicken cubes for 2 to 3 minutes, until cooked through.

3. Add the mixed vegetables and onion. Cook for 2 minutes.

4. Pour in the cream of chicken soup and 375 ml (1½ cups) water. Bring to a boil.

5. Separate the sections of flaky roll dough. Slice the rolls in half horizontally. Cover the chicken mixture with the roll halves.

6. Melt the remaining garlic butter in the microwave. Brush the rolls with melted butter.

7. Bake for 20 to 25 minutes.

⇨ Check out our recipe for homemade garlic butter on page 302!

HOMEMADE VERSION
Cream of Chicken Soup

Melt 60 ml (¼ cup) butter in a pot over medium heat. Cook 1 chopped onion for 1 minute. Sprinkle in 125 ml (½ cup) flour and stir. Add 500 ml (2 cups) chicken stock, 250 ml (1 cup) 15% cooking cream and 15 ml (1 tbsp) garlic powder. Season with salt and pepper. Bring to a boil, whisking, and let simmer until the mixture thickens.

1 **Chicken**
12 boneless thighs

2 **Garlic**
minced
15 ml (1 tbsp)

3 **Soy sauce**
125 ml (½ cup)

4 **Rice vinegar**
45 ml (3 tbsp)

5 **Honey**
60 ml (¼ cup)

ALSO NEEDED:
● **Flour**
60 ml (¼ cup)

Honey Garlic Chicken Thighs

Prep time **15 minutes** • Cook time **15 minutes** • Serves **4**

PER SERVING	
Calories	594
Protein	77 g
Fat	19 g
Carbohydrates	23 g
Fibre	0 g
Iron	4 mg
Calcium	38 mg
Sodium	1,387 mg

Preparation

1. Coat the chicken thighs in flour.

2. Heat a little olive oil in a frying pan over medium heat. Brown the chicken thighs for 2 to 3 minutes.

3. Add the garlic and cook for 30 seconds.

4. Pour the soy sauce, rice vinegar, honey and 60 ml (¼ cup) water into the pan. Bring to a boil and then cover and let simmer for 12 to 15 minutes over medium-low heat, until the chicken is no longer pink in the centre.

 You can replace the chicken thighs with chicken breasts!

SIDE DISH IDEA

Sautéed Snow Peas

Heat 15 ml (1 tbsp) canola oil in a pan over medium heat. Thinly slice 1 onion and ½ red pepper and cook for 1 minute. Add 300 g (⅔ lb) snow peas. Season with salt and pepper. Cook for 4 to 5 minutes, stirring frequently. Add 80 ml (⅓ cup) chopped peanuts and stir.

1 **Chicken**
4 skinless breasts

2 **Italian seasoning**
15 ml (1 tbsp)

3 **Bruschetta**
store-bought
1 container (340 g)

4 **Balsamic vinegar glaze**
30 ml (2 tbsp)

5 **Parmesan**
grated
180 ml (¾ cup)

Bruschetta Chicken

Prep time **15 minutes** · Cook time **20 minutes** · Serves **4**

Preparation

1. Preheat the oven to 205°C (400°F).

2. Season the chicken breasts with the Italian seasoning.

3. Heat a little olive oil in an ovenproof skillet over medium heat. Brown the breasts for 1 minute on each side.

4. Top the breasts with bruschetta. Drizzle with balsamic vinegar glaze and top with Parmesan.

5. Bake for 18 to 20 minutes, until the chicken is no longer pink in the centre.

⇨ Check out our recipe for homemade balsamic vinegar glaze on page 222.

PER SERVING	
Calories	415
Protein	40 g
Fat	21 g
Carbohydrates	13 g
Fibre	0 g
Iron	1 mg
Calcium	180 mg
Sodium	832 mg

HOMEMADE VERSION
Bruschetta

Seed and dice 3 Italian tomatoes. In a bowl, mix the tomatoes with 10 ml (2 tsp) minced garlic, 30 ml (2 tbsp) chopped fresh basil, 30 ml (2 tbsp) olive oil and 15 ml (1 tbsp) red wine vinegar. Season with salt and pepper.

1 **Chicken**
675 g (about 1½ lb)
skinless breasts,
cubed

2 **1 onion**
chopped

3 **Curry powder**
30 ml (2 tbsp)

4 **Diced tomatoes**
1 can (540 ml)

5 **Coconut milk**
1 can (398 ml)

ALSO NEEDED:
● **Garlic**
minced
15 ml (1 tbsp)

OPTIONAL:
● **Fresh cilantro**
15 ml (1 tbsp) leaves

Chicken Curry

Prep time **15 minutes** • Cook time **20 minutes** • Serves **4**

PER SERVING	
Calories	402
Protein	41 g
Fat	19 g
Carbohydrates	15 g
Fibre	2 g
Iron	7 mg
Calcium	86 mg
Sodium	321 mg

Preparation

1. Heat a little olive oil in a pot over medium heat. Brown the chicken cubes for 1 to 2 minutes.

2. Add the onion and garlic. Cook for 1 minute.

3. Add the curry powder and cook for 30 seconds, until fragrant.

4. Add the diced tomatoes and coconut milk. Stir. Bring to a boil and then let simmer for 18 to 20 minutes over medium-low heat, until the chicken is cooked through. Season with salt and pepper.

5. Garnish with cilantro before serving, if desired.

SIDE DISH IDEA

Coconut Lime Basmati Rice

Heat 15 ml (1 tbsp) canola oil in a pot over medium heat. Cook 125 ml (½ cup) chopped shallots for 1 minute. Add 250 ml (1 cup) basmati rice, rinsed and drained, 500 ml (2 cups) chicken stock and 125 ml (½ cup) unsweetened, shredded coconut. Stir. Bring to a boil and then cover and cook for 18 to 20 minutes. Add 15 ml (1 tbsp) lime zest and stir.

1 **Plain breadcrumbs**
125 ml (½ cup)

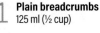

2 **Parmesan**
grated
80 ml (⅓ cup)

3 **Italian seasoning**
15 ml (1 tbsp)

4 **Mayonnaise**
60 ml (¼ cup)

5 **Chicken**
8 drumsticks

Crispy Parmesan Chicken Drumsticks

Prep time **15 minutes** • Cook time **40 minutes** • Serves **4**

PER SERVING	
Calories	477
Protein	52 g
Fat	22 g
Carbohydrates	12 g
Fibre	1 g
Iron	3 mg
Calcium	131 mg
Sodium	693 mg

Preparation

1. Preheat the oven to 205°C (400°F).

2. In a bowl, mix the breadcrumbs, Parmesan and Italian seasoning.

3. Spoon the mayonnaise into another bowl.

4. Dip the drumsticks into the mayonnaise and then coat them with the breadcrumb mixture.

5. Place the drumsticks on a baking sheet lined with parchment paper. Bake for 40 to 45 minutes, until the chicken is no longer pink in the centre.

 You can replace the chicken drumsticks with chicken legs!

SIDE DISH IDEA

Spinach, Tomato and Bocconcini Salad

In a salad bowl, combine 1 package (142 g) baby spinach with 18 cherry tomatoes cut in half, 1 container (200 g) bocconcini pearls, 1 small red onion, thinly sliced, and 125 ml (½ cup) Tuscan Italian dressing.

1 **Chicken**
4 skinless breasts,
cut into strips

2 **3 pepper halves**
various colours
thinly sliced

3 **Fajita seasoning**
1 packet (24 g)

4 **Mild salsa**
500 ml (2 cups)

5 **Tex-Mex shredded
cheese**
375 ml (1½ cups)

ALSO NEEDED:
- **1 small red onion**
thinly sliced

Chicken Fajita Casserole

Prep time **15 minutes** · Cook time **14 minutes** · Serves **4**

PER SERVING	
Calories	424
Protein	46 g
Fat	17 g
Carbohydrates	22 g
Fibre	5 g
Iron	3 mg
Calcium	90 mg
Sodium	1,511 mg

Preparation

1. Preheat the oven to 190°C (375°F).

2. Heat a little olive oil in a pot over medium heat. Brown the chicken strips for 1 to 2 minutes on each side.

3. Add the peppers and onion. Cook for 2 minutes.

4. Add the fajita seasoning and salsa. Stir and bring to a boil.

5. Transfer the chicken mixture to a baking dish. Top with cheese.

6. Bake for 10 to 12 minutes, until the chicken is no longer pink in the centre and the cheese is golden-brown.

 You can replace the Tex-Mex cheese with cheddar, Monterey Jack or mozzarella!

SIDE DISH IDEA

Lime Tortilla Chips

In a bowl, mix 15 ml (1 tbsp) olive oil with 15 ml (1 tbsp) lime zest and 15 ml (1 tbsp) chopped fresh cilantro. Brush 4 tortillas with the flavoured oil. Cut each tortilla into 8 triangles. Place the tortilla triangles on a baking sheet lined with parchment paper. Bake for 8 to 10 minutes at 190°C (375°F).

1 **Ground chicken**
450 g (1 lb)

2 **1 small zucchini**
shredded

3 **Feta**
crumbled
125 ml (½ cup)

4 **Plain breadcrumbs**
125 ml (½ cup)

5 **Fresh parsley**
chopped
60 ml (¼ cup)

ALSO NEEDED:
• **1 egg**

Zucchini and Feta Chicken Fritters

Prep time **15 minutes** • Cook time **12 minutes** • Serves **4 (8 fritters)**

PER SERVING	
2 fritters	
Calories	325
Protein	26 g
Fat	19 g
Carbohydrates	12 g
Fibre	1 g
Iron	2 mg
Calcium	146 mg
Sodium	375 mg

Preparation

1. In a bowl, mix the ground chicken with the zucchini, feta, breadcrumbs, parsley and egg. Season with salt and pepper.

2. Form 8 fritters, using about 80 ml (⅓ cup) of the mixture for each.

3. Heat a little olive oil in a frying pan over medium heat. Cook the fritters for 12 to 15 minutes, turning them several times, until they are no longer pink in the centre.

 You can replace the fresh parsley with 15 ml (1 tbsp) dried parsley!

A LITTLE EXTRA
Garlic Yogurt Sauce

Combine 180 ml (¾ cup) plain Greek yogurt, 45 ml (3 tbsp) mayonnaise, 15 ml (1 tbsp) minced garlic, 2 chopped green onions and 15 ml (1 tbsp) lemon zest. Season with salt and pepper.

Chicken
1 4 small, skinless breasts, cut into strips

Frozen stir-fry vegetable mix
2 500 ml (2 cups)

Soy sauce
3 45 ml (3 tbsp)

Oyster sauce
4 30 ml (2 tbsp)

Bean sprouts
5 500 ml (2 cups)

ALSO NEEDED:
● **Chicken stock**
80 ml (⅓ cup)

Chicken Chop Suey

Prep time **15 minutes** • Cook time **8 minutes** • Serves **4**

Preparation

1. Heat a little canola oil in a large frying pan over medium heat. Cook the chicken strips for 1 to 2 minutes on each side.

2. Add the vegetable blend and cook for another 5 to 7 minutes, until the chicken is no longer pink in the centre.

3. Pour in the soy sauce, oyster sauce and chicken stock. Stir and bring to a boil.

4. Add the bean sprouts. Season with pepper and cook for 30 seconds.

⇨ Check out our recipe for homemade Asian vegetable blend on page 25.

PER SERVING	
Calories	266
Protein	41 g
Fat	7 g
Carbohydrates	11 g
Fibre	2 g
Iron	2 mg
Calcium	63 mg
Sodium	1,072 mg

SIDE DISH IDEA

Green Onion Rice

Melt 15 ml (1 tbsp) butter in a pot over medium heat. Cook 15 ml (1 tbsp) minced ginger and 15 ml (1 tbsp) minced garlic for 1 minute. Add 250 ml (1 cup) basmati rice, rinsed and drained. Stir. Pour in 500 ml (2 cups) chicken stock and bring to a boil. Cover and cook for 18 to 20 minutes over low heat. Add 3 chopped green onions and stir.

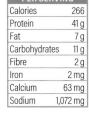

1 **Chicken**
4 skinless breasts

2 **Ranch dressing**
store-bought
180 ml (¾ cup)

3 **Sour cream (14%)**
125 ml (½ cup)

4 **1 small head broccoli**
cut into small florets

5 **Bacon**
10 slices, cooked
and chopped

Bacon Ranch Chicken

Prep time **15 minutes** • Cook time **17 minutes** • Serves **4**

PER SERVING	
Calories	504
Protein	41 g
Fat	35 g
Carbohydrates	6 g
Fibre	0 g
Iron	1 mg
Calcium	66 mg
Sodium	647 mg

Preparation

1. Preheat the oven to 190°C (375°F).

2. Heat a little olive oil in a large ovenproof skillet over medium heat. Brown the breasts for 1 minute on each side.

3. Pour the ranch dressing and sour cream into the skillet. Bring to a boil.

4. Distribute the broccoli around the breasts. Sprinkle with bacon. Cover and transfer the skillet to the oven. Bake for 15 to 18 minutes, until the chicken is no longer pink in the centre.

💡 You can replace the ranch dressing with Caesar or Thousand Island dressing!

HOMEMADE VERSION

Ranch Dressing

Mix 125 ml (½ cup) mayonnaise with 10 ml (2 tsp) minced garlic, 30 ml (2 tbsp) chopped fresh parsley, 15 ml (1 tbsp) chopped fresh chives and 15 ml (1 tbsp) fresh lemon juice. Season with salt and pepper.

1 **Flour**
45 ml (3 tbsp)

2 **Chicken**
8 cutlets, 80 g
(about 2¾ oz) each

3 **Capers**
15 ml (1 tbsp)

4 **Lemon juice**
30 ml (2 tbsp)

5 **Butter**
45 ml (3 tbsp)

Chicken Piccata

Prep time **15 minutes** • Cook time **5 minutes** • Serves **4**

Preparation

1. Coat the chicken cutlets in flour.

2. Heat a little olive oil in a frying pan over medium heat. Cook the cutlets for 2 to 3 minutes on each side, until the chicken is no longer pink in the centre.

3. Add the capers, lemon juice and butter to the pan. Stir. Cook for 1 minute.

 This recipe is also great with chicken breasts. Simply cut four breasts in half widthwise, place them between two pieces of plastic wrap and flatten them with a rolling pin.

PER SERVING	
Calories	324
Protein	37 g
Fat	17 g
Carbohydrates	5 g
Fibre	0 g
Iron	1 mg
Calcium	17 mg
Sodium	194 mg

SIDE DISH IDEA

Creamy Parmesan Gemelli

Cook 750 ml (3 cups) gemelli pasta *al dente* in a pot of boiling, salted water. Drain and set aside. In the same pot, add 250 ml (1 cup) 15% cooking cream and ½ package (250 g) cream cheese. Bring to a boil, stirring constantly. Add 125 ml (½ cup) grated Parmesan and 30 ml (2 tbsp) chopped fresh chives. Season with salt and pepper. Let simmer for 2 minutes. Add the gemelli and reheat for 1 minute, stirring.

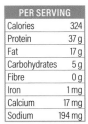

1 **Chicken**
4 skinless breasts

2 **Italian seasoning**
15 ml (1 tbsp)

3 **Marinara sauce**
375 ml (1½ cups)

4 **Pepperoni**
20 to 25 small
slices

5 **Italian shredded
cheese blend**
250 ml (1 cup)

OPTIONAL:
● **Fresh basil**
30 ml (2 tbsp) leaves

Pepperoni and Cheese Chicken

Prep time **15 minutes** • Cook time **22 minutes** • Serves **4**

PER SERVING	
Calories	373
Protein	43 g
Fat	18 g
Carbohydrates	9 g
Fibre	3 g
Iron	1 mg
Calcium	225 mg
Sodium	652 mg

Preparation

1. Preheat the oven to 190°C (375°F).

2. Season the chicken breasts with Italian seasoning.

3. Heat a little olive oil in a large ovenproof skillet over medium heat. Brown the chicken breasts for 2 to 3 minutes on each side. Set aside on a plate.

4. Pour the marinara sauce into the same skillet. Top with half of the pepperoni and then place the chicken breasts back in the skillet. Cover with cheese and the remaining pepperoni.

5. Bake for 16 to 20 minutes, until the chicken is no longer pink in the centre.

6. Brown the cheese under the broiler for 2 to 3 minutes.

7. Garnish with basil before serving if desired.

SIDE DISH IDEA

Parmesan Sticks

In a bowl, mix 125 ml (½ cup) grated Parmesan with 15 ml (1 tbsp) chopped fresh thyme, 5 ml (1 tsp) garlic powder and 5 ml (1 tsp) onion powder. On a floured surface, stretch out 1 ball of pizza dough (255 g) into a rectangle, 20 cm x 10 cm (8 in x 4 in). Brush the dough with 15 ml (1 tbsp) olive oil and sprinkle with Parmesan. Cut the dough into 12 strips, widthwise. Place the strips of dough on a baking sheet lined with parchment paper. Bake for 15 to 18 minutes at 205°C (400°F).

1 **Chicken**
4 skinless breasts

2 **Thousand Island dressing**
store-bought
180 ml (¾ cup)

3 **Bacon**
8 slices, cooked

4 **1 head romaine lettuce**
chopped

5 **18 cherry tomatoes**
cut in half

OPTIONAL:
● **4 green onions**
chopped

Grilled Chicken BLT Salad

Prep time **15 minutes** · Cook time **15 minutes** · Serves **4**

PER SERVING	
Calories	456
Protein	39 g
Fat	27 g
Carbohydrates	13 g
Fibre	3 g
Iron	2 mg
Calcium	40 mg
Sodium	661 mg

Preparation

1. Brush the chicken breasts with a quarter of the dressing.

2. Heat a little olive oil in a frying pan over medium heat. Cook the chicken breasts for 15 to 18 minutes, turning them over several times, until the chicken is no longer pink in the centre.

3. Slice the chicken breasts. Chop the bacon slices.

4. Distribute the lettuce, cherry tomatoes and bacon into four bowls. Top with the chicken strips, remaining dressing, and green onions if desired.

 You can replace the Thousand Island dressing with the dressing of your choice!

── HOMEMADE VERSION ──
Thousand Island Dressing

Mix 125 ml (½ cup) mayonnaise with 30 ml (2 tbsp) relish, 30 ml (2 tbsp) ketchup, 2 chopped green onions, 15 ml (1 tbsp) fresh lemon juice and 15 ml (1 tbsp) Worcestershire sauce.

1 **Cream cheese**
softened
½ container (250 g)

2 **3 artichoke hearts**
chopped

3 **Baby spinach**
250 ml (1 cup)

4 **Italian shredded cheese blend**
125 ml (½ cup)

5 **Chicken**
4 skinless breasts

Artichoke Dip-Stuffed Chicken

Prep time **15 minutes** • Cook time **20 minutes** • Serves **4**

Preparation

1. Preheat the oven to 205°C (400°F).

2. In a bowl, mix the cream cheese with the artichoke hearts, spinach and shredded cheese. Season with salt and pepper.

3. Slice the chicken breasts in half horizontally, without cutting all the way through.

4. Stuff the chicken breasts with the cream cheese mixture. Use toothpicks to keep the breasts closed.

5. Heat a little olive oil in an ovenproof skillet over medium heat. Brown the breasts for 1 minute on each side.

6. Transfer to the oven and bake for 18 to 20 minutes, until the chicken is no longer pink in the centre.

PER SERVING	
Calories	353
Protein	40 g
Fat	20 g
Carbohydrates	4 g
Fibre	1 g
Iron	1 mg
Calcium	120 mg
Sodium	440 mg

SIDE DISH IDEA

Lemon Couscous Salad

In a bowl, mix 250 ml (1 cup) couscous with 30 ml (2 tbsp) olive oil. Season with salt and pepper. Pour in 250 ml (1 cup) boiling water. Cover and let rest for 5 minutes before fluffing it with a fork. Let cool. Add ½ English cucumber, diced, 3 Italian tomatoes, diced, 60 ml (¼ cup) chopped fresh parsley and 30 ml (2 tbsp) fresh lemon juice to the bowl. Stir.

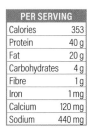

1 **California blend frozen vegetables**
750 ml (3 cups)

2 **Chicken**
4 skinless breasts, cubed

3 **Alfredo sauce**
store-bought
625 ml (2½ cups)

4 **White rice**
cooked
500 ml (2 cups)

5 **Vegetable crackers**
crushed into breadcrumbs
250 ml (1 cup)

OPTIONAL:
● **Fresh basil**
chopped
45 ml (3 tbsp)

Chicken and Rice Casserole

Prep time **15 minutes** • Cook time **24 minutes** • Serves **4**

PER SERVING	
Calories	664
Protein	42 g
Fat	25 g
Carbohydrates	62 g
Fibre	5 g
Iron	2 mg
Calcium	105 mg
Sodium	1,463 mg

Preparation

1. Preheat the oven to 205°C (400°F).

2. Cook the vegetable blend in a pot of boiling, salted water for 3 minutes. Drain.

3. Heat a little olive oil in a frying pan over medium heat. Brown the chicken cubes for 1 to 2 minutes.

4. Pour in the Alfredo sauce and bring to a boil.

5. Remove from heat and add the vegetables, cooked rice, and basil if desired. Stir.

6. Grease a 33 cm x 23 cm (13 in x 9 in) baking dish and pour the chicken mixture into it. Cover with cracker breadcrumbs.

7. Bake for 20 to 25 minutes, until the chicken is cooked through and the breadcrumbs are golden-brown.

 You can replace the vegetable crackers with any other type of cracker!

HOMEMADE VERSION
Alfredo Sauce

Place 125 ml (½ cup) butter and 500 ml (2 cups) 15% cooking cream in a pot. Bring to a boil. Season with salt and pepper. Remove from heat. Gradually add 375 ml (1½ cups) grated Parmesan, stirring constantly, until the Parmesan is melted.

1 **Sweet and sour sauce**
180 ml (¾ cup)

2 **Chicken**
4 skinless breasts, cubed

3 **¼ pineapple**
cubed

4 **1 red pepper**
cubed

5 **1 small red onion**
cubed

Sweet and Sour Chicken Skewers

Prep time **15 minutes** · Cook time **18 minutes** · Serves **4**

PER SERVING	
Calories	313
Protein	35 g
Fat	4 g
Carbohydrates	33 g
Fibre	2 g
Iron	1 mg
Calcium	27 mg
Sodium	131 mg

Preparation

1. Preheat the oven to 205°C (400°F).

2. In a bowl, combine a third of the sauce with the chicken and pineapple cubes.

3. Thread the cubes of chicken, pineapple, pepper and onion onto 4 skewers, alternating between ingredients.

4. Place the skewers on a baking sheet lined with parchment paper. Bake for 18 to 20 minutes, turning the skewers over at the halfway point, until the chicken is no longer pink in the centre.

5. Serve the skewers with the remaining sauce.

⇨ Check out our recipe for homemade sweet and sour sauce on page 80.

SIDE DISH IDEA

Bacon Rice Pilaf

Heat 15 ml (1 tbsp) olive oil in a pot over medium heat. Place 10 slices of pre-cooked bacon, chopped, 250 ml (1 cup) long grain white rice and 1 chopped onion in the pot. Cook for 1 minute, stirring. Add 500 ml (2 cups) chicken stock. Season with salt and pepper. Bring to a boil and then cover and cook for 20 to 25 minutes, until the liquid is completely absorbed.

1 **Chicken**
4 skinless breasts

2 **Cooking cream (15%)**
500 ml (2 cups)

3 **Basil pesto**
45 ml (3 tbsp)

4 **2 Italian tomatoes**
seeded and diced

5 **2 small zucchinis**
cut into small cubes

ALSO NEEDED:
● **1 onion**
chopped

OPTIONAL:
● **Parmesan**
grated
125 ml (½ cup)

Creamy Pesto Chicken

Prep time **15 minutes** • Cook time **18 minutes** • Serves **4**

PER SERVING	
Calories	550
Protein	41 g
Fat	37 g
Carbohydrates	14 g
Fibre	2 g
Iron	1 mg
Calcium	257 mg
Sodium	369 mg

Preparation

1. Heat a little olive oil in a frying pan over medium heat. Brown the chicken breasts for 1 to 2 minutes on each side.

2. Add the onion and cook for 1 minute.

3. Add the cream and pesto. Bring to a boil.

4. Add the tomatoes and zucchinis. Season with salt and pepper. Cover and cook for 15 to 18 minutes, until the chicken is no longer pink in the centre.

5. Top with Parmesan before serving if desired.

⇨ **Check out our recipe for homemade basil pesto on page 248.**

SIDE DISH IDEA

Almond Butter Linguine

Cook 350 g (about ¾ lb) linguine *al dente* in a pot of boiling, salted water. Drain and set aside. In the same pot, heat 30 ml (2 tbsp) olive oil over medium heat. Add 60 ml (¼ cup) almond butter, 60 ml (¼ cup) chopped fresh parsley and the linguine. Season with salt and pepper. Reheat for 1 minute, stirring.

1 **Chicken**
4 skinless breasts

2 **2 small red onions**
finely diced

3 **Barbecue sauce**
250 ml (1 cup)

4 **Chicken stock**
125 ml (½ cup)

5 **Tex-Mex shredded cheese**
500 ml (2 cups)

OPTIONAL:
● **Fresh thyme**
chopped
10 ml (2 tsp)

Cheesy Barbecue Chicken Breasts

Prep time **15 minutes** · Cook time **18 minutes** · Serves **4**

PER SERVING	
Calories	594
Protein	49 g
Fat	27 g
Carbohydrates	36 g
Fibre	1 g
Iron	2 mg
Calcium	450 mg
Sodium	1,056 mg

Preparation

1. Preheat the oven to 205°C (400°F).

2. Heat a little olive oil in an ovenproof skillet over medium heat. Brown the breasts for 1 minute on each side.

3. Add the onions and cook for 1 to 2 minutes.

4. Pour in the barbecue sauce and stock. Bring to a boil.

5. Top the mixture with the cheese blend. Transfer to the oven and bake for 15 to 18 minutes, until the chicken is no longer pink in the centre.

6. Garnish with thyme before serving if desired.

 You can replace the Tex-Mex cheese blend with a blend of sharp yellow cheddar and Monterey Jack!

SIDE DISH IDEA

Sautéed Peppers

Slice 3 peppers of various colours and 1 small red onion. Heat 15 ml (1 tbsp) olive oil in a frying pan over medium heat. Cook the peppers and onion for 3 to 4 minutes. Add 125 ml (½ cup) sliced almonds and 60 ml (¼ cup) chopped fresh parsley. Season with salt and pepper. Heat for 1 minute.

1 **16 small asparagus spears**
cut in half

2 **Chicken**
8 small cutlets

3 **Dijon mustard**
30 ml (2 tbsp)

4 **Prosciutto**
8 slices

5 **Swiss cheese**
8 slices

Asparagus and Prosciutto Chicken Rolls

Prep time **15 minutes** • Cook time **20 minutes** • Serves **4**

PER SERVING	
Calories	337
Protein	44 g
Fat	17 g
Carbohydrates	4 g
Fibre	1 g
Iron	2 mg
Calcium	126 mg
Sodium	1,548 mg

Preparation

1. Preheat the oven to 205°C (400°F).

2. Cook the asparagus for 2 minutes in a pot of boiling, salted water. Drain.

3. Brush the cutlets with mustard.

4. Place 1 slice of prosciutto and 1 slice of cheese on each cutlet. Top with asparagus. Roll the cutlets around the asparagus. Secure the rolls with toothpicks.

5. Heat a little olive oil in an ovenproof skillet over medium heat. Brown the rolls for 1 to 2 minutes on each side.

6. Transfer to the oven and bake for 18 to 20 minutes, until the chicken is no longer pink in the centre.

 You can replace the chicken with pork or veal cutlets!

SIDE DISH IDEA

Sun-Dried Tomato Salad

Pour 125 ml (½ cup) maple mustard dressing into a salad bowl. Add 1 package of spring mix lettuce (142 g), 4 sun-dried tomatoes, chopped, 2 green onions, chopped, and 80 ml (⅓ cup) sunflower seeds. Stir.

1 **Chicken**
4 skinless breasts,
cut into strips

2 **3 pepper halves**
various colours
sliced

3 **Stir-fry sauce**
store-bought
125 ml (½ cup)

4 **Cashew nuts**
180 ml (¾ cup)

5 **16 snow peas**

ALSO NEEDED:
• **Garlic**
2 cloves, minced

Cashew Chicken Stir-Fry

Prep time **15 minutes** • Cook time **8 minutes** • Serves **4**

Preparation

1. Heat a little olive oil in a frying pan over medium heat. Brown the chicken strips for 1 to 2 minutes on each side.

2. Add the peppers and garlic. Cook for 1 to 2 minutes.

3. Add the sauce, cashews and snow peas. Stir. Bring to a boil and then cook for 5 to 6 minutes over medium-low heat, until the chicken is no longer pink in the centre.

You can replace the classic stir-fry sauce with the stir-fry sauce flavour of your choice (General Tso, orange ginger, hoisin garlic, etc.).

PER SERVING	
Calories	426
Protein	39 g
Fat	20 g
Carbohydrates	24 g
Fibre	2 g
Iron	3 mg
Calcium	34 mg
Sodium	701 mg

HOMEMADE VERSION

Stir-Fry Sauce

In a pot, mix 180 ml (¾ cup) teriyaki marinade sauce with 15 ml (1 tbsp) minced ginger, 10 ml (2 tsp) minced garlic and 5 ml (1 tsp) cornstarch. Bring to a boil, whisking.

1 **Chicken**
450 g (1 lb) skinless
breasts, diced

2 **Frozen diced
vegetable mix**
500 ml (2 cups)

3 **Condensed cream
of chicken soup**
2 cans (284 ml
each)

4 **Chicken stock**
750 ml (3 cups)

5 **Rice**
cooked
375 ml (1½ cups)

OPTIONAL:
● **Fresh parsley**
chopped
60 ml (¼ cup)

Chicken and Rice Soup

Prep time **15 minutes** · Cook time **12 minutes** · Serves **4**

PER SERVING	
Calories	459
Protein	33 g
Fat	19 g
Carbohydrates	37 g
Fibre	4 g
Iron	2 mg
Calcium	65 mg
Sodium	1,885 mg

Preparation

1. Heat a little olive oil in a pot over medium heat. Cook the chicken for 4 to 5 minutes, until it is no longer pink in the centre.

2. Add the vegetable mix and cook for 2 to 3 minutes.

3. Add the cream of chicken soup and stock. Stir. Bring to a boil and let simmer for 5 minutes over medium-low heat.

4. Add the cooked rice. Heat for 1 minute.

5. Garnish with parsley before serving if desired.

⇨ Check out our recipe for a homemade diced vegetable mix for spaghetti on page 25.

SIDE DISH IDEA

Cheese Croutons

Cut ½ baguette into 12 slices. Place the bread slices on a baking sheet lined with parchment paper. Sprinkle the slices with 15 ml (1 tbsp) chicken seasoning. Top with 250 ml (1 cup) shredded Swiss cheese. Bake for 10 to 12 minutes at 190°C (375°F).

1 **Chicken**
4 legs

2 **Greek seasoning**
30 ml (2 tbsp)

3 **4 potatoes**
cut into wedges

4 **Cherry tomatoes**
1 container (190 g)

5 **1 lemon**
cut into wedges

Sheet Pan Greek Chicken Legs

Prep time **15 minutes** • Cook time **40 minutes** • Serves **4**

PER SERVING	
Calories	590
Protein	34 g
Fat	16 g
Carbohydrates	80 g
Fibre	9 g
Iron	6 mg
Calcium	156 mg
Sodium	1,435 mg

Preparation

1. Preheat the oven to 205°C (400°F).

2. Place the chicken legs on a baking sheet lined with parchment paper. Sprinkle the legs with half of the Greek seasoning.

3. Spread the potatoes, tomatoes, lemon, onions, and olives, if desired, around the legs. Sprinkle with the remaining Greek seasoning. Drizzle with olive oil.

4. Bake for 40 to 45 minutes, until the chicken is no longer pink in the centre.

 You can replace the chicken legs with chicken drumsticks!

A LITTLE EXTRA
Feta Tzatziki

Mix 180 ml (¾ cup) plain Greek yogurt with 15 ml (1 tbsp) lemon zest, 10 ml (2 tsp) minced garlic, 30 ml (2 tbsp) chopped fresh parsley, 125 ml (½ cup) grated, pressed cucumber and 80 ml (⅓ cup) crumbled feta. Season with salt and pepper, and stir.

ALSO NEEDED:
● **2 small red onions**
cut into wedges

OPTIONAL:
● **Olives**
250 ml (1 cup)

1 **Chicken**
3 skinless breasts

2 **Salad seasoning**
15 ml (1 tbsp)

3 **Flour**
125 ml (½ cup)

4 **2 eggs**

5 **Corn Flakes cereal**
finely crushed
250 ml (1 cup)

Cereal-Crusted Chicken Tenders

Prep time **15 minutes** · Cook time **25 minutes** · Serves **4 portions**

PER SERVING	
Calories	367
Protein	33 g
Fat	10 g
Carbohydrates	32 g
Fibre	1 g
Iron	6 mg
Calcium	21 mg
Sodium	216 mg

Preparation

1. Preheat the oven to 190°C (375°F).

2. Cut each chicken breast into 6 cubes.

3. In a bowl, mix the chicken cubes with the salad seasoning.

4. Set out three shallow bowls. Put the flour in the first. Beat the eggs in the second. Pour the cereal in the third.

5. Coat the chicken cubes in flour and shake to remove the excess. Dip the chicken cubes into the beaten eggs, and then coat them with cereal.

6. Place the chicken tenders on a baking sheet lined with parchment paper. Drizzle with olive oil.

7. Bake for 25 to 30 minutes, until the chicken is no longer pink in the centre.

 You can replace the corn flakes with rice cereal or panko breadcrumbs.

┌ **A LITTLE EXTRA**
Honey Barbecue Sauce

Mix 125 ml (½ cup) mayonnaise with 60 ml (¼ cup) barbecue sauce, 15 ml (1 tbsp) honey and 15 ml (1 tbsp) Dijon mustard.

PORK

Mediterranean-style stuffed tenderloin,
pork chops with mushrooms, ham au gratin,
sausage-stuffed zucchini: rediscover all
the different and delicious cuts of pork out
there! Affordable and quick to prepare, it's
the perfect choice for busy weeknight meals!

1 **Pork**
675 g (1½ lb)
tenderloin

2 **Dijon mustard**
30 ml (2 tbsp)

3 **Honey**
30 ml (2 tbsp)

4 **Cooking
cream (15%)**
250 ml (1 cup)

5 **Fresh rosemary**
chopped
10 ml (2 tsp)

ALSO NEEDED:
● **1 onion**
chopped

Honey Dijon Pork Tenderloin

Prep time **15 minutes** • Cook time **20 minutes** • Serves **4**

PER SERVING	
Calories	380
Protein	39 g
Fat	17 g
Carbohydrates	15 g
Fibre	1 g
Iron	2 mg
Calcium	76 mg
Sodium	301 mg

Preparation

1. Trim the pork tenderloin by removing the silver skin.

2. Heat a little olive oil in a frying pan over medium heat. Brown the tenderloin for 2 to 3 minutes on all sides.

3. Add the onion and cook for 1 minute.

4. Add the Dijon mustard, honey, cream and rosemary. Season with salt and pepper. Bring to a boil, and then cover and cook over medium-low heat for 17 to 20 minutes.

5. Transfer the tenderloin to a plate and cover loosely with aluminum foil. Let rest for 5 minutes before slicing.

6. Serve the tenderloin with the remaining sauce from the pan.

 You can replace the rosemary with the same amount of fresh thyme or with 2.5 ml (½ tsp) of your favourite dried herbs!

SIDE DISH IDEA

Roasted Paprika Creamer Potatoes

In a bowl, mix 30 ml (2 tbsp) olive oil with 15 ml (1 tbsp) paprika, 15 ml (1 tbsp) minced garlic, 1 chopped onion and 450 g (1 lb) creamer potatoes cut in half. Season with salt and pepper. Spread the prepared ingredients on a baking sheet lined with parchment paper. Bake for 20 to 25 minutes at 205°C (400°F).

1 **Smoked ham**
cubed
300 g (⅔ lb)

2 **½ pineapple**
cubed

3 **Long grain
white rice**
250 ml (1 cup)

4 **Sweet and
sour sauce**
store-bought
180 ml (¾ cup)

5 **3 green onions**
chopped

Pineapple and Ham Rice

Prep time **15 minutes** • Cook time **21 minutes** • Serves **4**

PER SERVING	
Calories	431
Protein	14 g
Fat	8 g
Carbohydrates	77 g
Fibre	3 g
Iron	1 mg
Calcium	51 mg
Sodium	889 mg

Preparation

1. Heat a little canola oil in a pot over medium heat. Cook the cubed ham and pineapple for 1 to 2 minutes.

2. Add the rice, sweet and sour sauce and 310 ml (1¼ cups) of water. Stir. Bring to a boil, and then cover and let simmer over low heat for 20 to 25 minutes, until the liquid is completely absorbed.

3. Add the green onions to the pot and stir.

HOMEMADE VERSION
Sweet and Sour Sauce

In a bowl, mix 60 ml (¼ cup) maple syrup with 30 ml (2 tbsp) soy sauce, 30 ml (2 tbsp) oyster sauce, 10 ml (2 tsp) minced garlic, 125 ml (½ cup) orange juice and 45 ml (3 tbsp) ketchup. Heat in the microwave for 1 minute.

1 **8 Italian sausages**

2 **2 zucchinis**
cut into half rounds

3 **1 small red onion**
cut into wedges

4 **Italian vinaigrette**
125 ml (½ cup)

5 **Italian shredded
cheese blend**
500 ml (2 cups)

Sheet Pan Cheesy Italian Sausage

Prep time **15 minutes** • Cook time **22 minutes** • Serves **4**

PER SERVING	
Calories	648
Protein	36 g
Fat	46 g
Carbohydrates	24 g
Fibre	1 g
Iron	2 mg
Calcium	375 mg
Sodium	1,734 mg

Preparation

1. Preheat the oven to 205°C (400°F).

2. Place the sausages on a baking sheet lined with parchment paper. Bake for 8 to 10 minutes.

3. Remove the sausages from the oven and cut into rounds.

4. Spread the sausage, zucchini and onion on the baking sheet. Drizzle with vinaigrette. Season with salt and pepper. Bake for 12 minutes.

5. Remove the baking sheet from the oven and top with cheese. Cook for another 2 to 3 minutes.

SIDE DISH IDEA

Garlic Butter Baguette

In a microwave-safe bowl, melt 80 ml (⅓ cup) butter in the microwave. Add 15 ml (1 tbsp) minced garlic, 30 ml (2 tbsp) chopped fresh parsley and 15 ml (1 tbsp) Italian seasoning in the bowl. Season with salt and pepper, and stir. Cut ½ ciabatta baguette in half lengthwise. Place the baguette halves on a baking sheet lined with parchment paper and brush them with garlic butter. Bake for 10 to 12 minutes at 205°C (400°F). Remove from the oven and then cut the baguette into pieces.

1 **Pork**
4 pork chops, 180 g
(about ⅓ lb) each

2 **Whole-grain mustard**
30 ml (2 tbsp)

3 **2 onions**
chopped

4 **2 Gala apples**
cut into wedges

5 **Apple juice**
180 ml (¾ cup)

OPTIONAL:
● **Fresh thyme**
chopped
15 ml (1 tbsp)

Apple Pork Chops

Prep time **15 minutes** • Cook time **14 minutes** • Serves **4**

Preparation

1. Preheat the oven to 205°C (400°F).

2. Heat a little olive oil in an ovenproof skillet over medium heat. Brown the pork chops for 1 minute on each side.

3. Add the mustard, onions, apple wedges, apple juice, and thyme if desired. Season with salt and pepper, and stir. Bring to a boil, then transfer to the oven and bake for another 12 to 15 minutes.

 You can also replace the whole-grain mustard with Dijon or honey mustard!

PER SERVING	
Calories	381
Protein	42 g
Fat	12 g
Carbohydrates	25 g
Fibre	4 g
Iron	1 mg
Calcium	45 mg
Sodium	272 mg

SIDE DISH IDEA

Kale Salad

In a salad bowl, mix 15 ml (1 tbsp) Dijon mustard with 15 ml (1 tbsp) apple cider vinegar and 45 ml (3 tbsp) olive oil. Season with salt and pepper. Add 1 bunch of kale cut into pieces, 125 ml (½ cup) walnuts and 60 ml (¼ cup) grated Parmesan. Stir.

1 Pork
675 g (1½ lb)
tenderloin

2 Feta
crumbled
125 ml (½ cup)

3 Baby spinach
chopped
375 ml (1½ cups)

**4 Sun-dried
tomatoes**
diced
125 ml (½ cup)

5 Greek seasoning
15 ml (1 tbsp)

Mediterranean Stuffed Pork Tenderloin

Prep time **15 minutes** • Cook time **20 minutes** • Serves **4**

PER SERVING	
Calories	329
Protein	42 g
Fat	14 g
Carbohydrates	8 g
Fibre	1 g
Iron	4 mg
Calcium	154 mg
Sodium	637 mg

Preparation

1. Preheat the oven to 205°C (400°F).

2. Trim the pork tenderloin by removing the silver skin.

3. Slice the tenderloins in half lengthwise, without cutting all the way through.

4. In a bowl, mix the feta with the spinach and sun-dried tomatoes.

5. Open the tenderloin like a book and stuff with the feta mixture. Close it back up and tie with string.

6. Heat a little olive oil in an ovenproof skillet over medium heat. Brown the tenderloin for 2 to 3 minutes on all sides.

7. Sprinkle the tenderloin with Greek seasoning. Transfer to the oven and bake for 18 to 20 minutes.

SIDE DISH IDEA

Lemon Herb Couscous

In a bowl, mix 375 ml (1½ cups) couscous with 15 ml (1 tbsp) olive oil, 60 ml (¼ cup) chopped fresh parsley, 30 ml (2 tbsp) chopped fresh oregano and 15 ml (1 tbsp) lemon zest. Season with salt and pepper. Bring 375 ml (1½ cups) chicken stock and 30 ml (2 tbsp) fresh lemon juice to boil in a pot. Pour the stock into the bowl and stir. Cover and let the couscous steam for 5 minutes. Fluff the couscous with a fork.

1 **Ground pork**
450 g (1 lb)

2 **1 onion**
chopped

3 **Ginger**
chopped
15 ml (1 tbsp)

4 **Coleslaw
vegetable mix**
500 ml (2 cups)

5 **Soy sauce**
60 ml (¼ cup)

ALSO NEEDED:
● **Garlic**
chopped
15 ml (1 tbsp)

OPTIONAL:
● **Fresh cilantro**
30 ml (2 tbsp) leaves

Egg Roll in a Bowl

Prep time **15 minutes** • Cook time **10 minutes** • Serves **4**

PER SERVING	
Calories	322
Protein	24 g
Fat	21 g
Carbohydrates	9 g
Fibre	2 g
Iron	4 mg
Calcium	52 mg
Sodium	978 mg

Preparation

1. Heat a little olive oil in a frying pan over medium heat. Cook the ground pork for 8 to 10 minutes, breaking up the meat with a wooden spoon, until it is no longer pink.

2. Add the onion and garlic. Stir. Cook for 1 minute.

3. Add the coleslaw vegetable mix and soy sauce. Stir. Bring to a boil and then cook for 1 to 2 minutes.

4. Garnish with cilantro before serving, if desired.

💡 You can replace the coleslaw vegetable mix with the same amount of shredded cabbage!

A LITTLE EXTRA

Plum Sauce

Heat 15 ml (1 tbsp) canola oil in a pot over medium heat. Cook 1 chopped onion, 15 ml (1 tbsp) minced garlic and 15 ml (1 tbsp) minced ginger for 1 minute. Add 4 large diced plums and stir. Cook for 2 minutes. Add 15 ml (1 tbsp) honey, 30 ml (2 tbsp) balsamic vinegar and 180 ml (¾ cup) vegetable stock. Bring to a boil, and let simmer for 5 to 6 minutes over medium-low heat. Use an immersion blender to blend the sauce. Use a fine strainer to filter the sauce.

1 Pork
4 pork chops, 180 g
(about ⅓ lb) each

2 Mushrooms
sliced
1 container (227 g)

3 1 onion
chopped

4 Condensed cream
of mushroom
soup
1 can (284 ml)

5 2% milk
310 ml (1¼ cups)

ALSO NEEDED:
● **Garlic**
chopped
15 ml (1 tbsp)

Mushroom Pork Chops

Prep time **15 minutes** • Cook time **15 minutes** • Serves **4**

Preparation

1. Heat a little olive oil in a frying pan over medium heat. Brown the chops for 1 minute on each side.

2. Add the mushrooms, onion and garlic. Cook for 1 minute.

3. Add the cream of mushroom soup and milk. Season with salt and pepper, and stir. Bring to a boil, and then cover and cook for 12 to 15 minutes.

PER SERVING	
Calories	421
Protein	47 g
Fat	18 g
Carbohydrates	18 g
Fibre	2 g
Iron	2 mg
Calcium	146 mg
Sodium	761 mg

SIDE DISH IDEA

Buttered Green Beans

Cut 450 g (1 lb) green beans into pieces and cook in a pot of boiling, salted water for 4 to 5 minutes. Drain. In a frying pan, melt 30 ml (2 tbsp) butter over medium heat. Cook 2 chopped shallots and 2 minced cloves of garlic for 1 minute. Add the green beans. Season with salt and pepper. Cook for 1 to 2 minutes, stirring.

1 **Pork**
675 g (1½ lb)
tenderloin

2 **Brown sugar**
30 ml (2 tbsp)

3 **Smoked sweet paprika**
15 ml (1 tbsp)

4 **Bacon**
450 g (1 lb)

5 **Maple syrup**
45 ml (3 tbsp)

Caramelized Bacon-Wrapped Pork Tenderloin

Prep time 15 minutes • Cook time 30 minutes • Serves 4

PER SERVING	
Calories	633
Protein	52 g
Fat	40 g
Carbohydrates	15 g
Fibre	1 g
Iron	3 mg
Calcium	33 mg
Sodium	788 mg

Preparation

1. Preheat the oven to 205°C (400°F).

2. Trim the pork tenderloin by removing the silver skin.

3. Mix the sugar and paprika together in a bowl. Season with salt and pepper.

4. Rub the pork tenderloin with the sugar mixture.

5. Arrange the bacon slices on your work surface so that they are slightly overlapping. Place the pork tenderloin in the middle of the slices. Wrap the bacon slices around the tenderloin.

6. Place the tenderloin on a baking sheet lined with parchment paper with the joins of the bacon slices against the pan. Brush the tenderloin with maple syrup.

7. Bake for 30 to 35 minutes.

8. Remove the tenderloin from the oven and transfer to a plate. Cover it loosely with aluminum foil. Let rest for 5 minutes before slicing.

SIDE DISH IDEA

Ranch Salad

In a salad bowl, mix 1 head of curly leaf lettuce, shredded, with 12 cherry tomatoes in various colours cut in half, 1 small red onion cut into thin rings, 60 ml (¼ cup) sliced almonds and 125 ml (½ cup) ranch dressing.

1 **Condensed cream
of chicken soup**
2 cans (284 ml each)

2 **3 potatoes**
peeled and cubed

3 **Corn kernels**
375 ml (1½ cups)

4 **Ham**
cubed
450 g (1 lb)

5 **Frozen
for soup
vegetables**
500 ml (2 cups)

Ham and Corn Chowder

Prep time **15 minutes** • Cook time **15 minutes** • Serves **4**

PER SERVING	
Calories	496
Protein	30 g
Fat	19 g
Carbohydrates	63 g
Fibre	7 g
Iron	3 mg
Calcium	292 mg
Sodium	2,326 mg

Preparation

1. Pour the cream of chicken soup and 750 ml (3 cups) of water in a pot. Bring to a boil, whisking.

2. Add the potatoes, corn, ham and mixed vegetables. Stir. Cook for 15 to 18 minutes, until the vegetables are tender.

 You can replace the water with the same amount of milk for an even creamier chowder!

SIDE DISH IDEA

Thyme Croutons

In a bowl, mix 15 ml (1 tbsp) olive oil with 15 ml (1 tbsp) melted butter and 15 ml (1 tbsp) chopped fresh thyme. Cut ½ baguette into 12 slices. Brush the slices with the flavoured oil. Place the slices on a baking sheet lined with parchment paper. Bake for 8 to 10 minutes at 180°C (350°F).

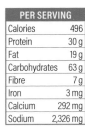

1 **4 zucchinis**

2 **4 Italian sausages**

3 **2 Italian tomatoes**
seeded and diced

4 **Pizza sauce**
250 ml (1 cup)

5 **Mozzarella**
shredded
375 ml (1½ cups)

ALSO NEEDED:
• **1 onion**
chopped

Sausage-Stuffed Zucchinis

Prep time **15 minutes** • Cook time **20 minutes** • Serves **4**

PER SERVING	
Calories	417
Protein	24 g
Fat	25 g
Carbohydrates	24 g
Fibre	4 g
Iron	2 mg
Calcium	327 mg
Sodium	1,150 mg

Preparation

1. Preheat the oven to 205°C (400°F).

2. Cut off the tops of the zucchinis, lengthwise. Spoon out the flesh of the zucchini, leaving a width of 1 cm (½ in) of zucchini around the edge.

3. Remove the casing from the sausages.

4. In a bowl, mix the sausage meat with the tomatoes and onion.

5. Stuff the zucchinis with the sausage mixture.

6. Place the stuffed zucchinis on a baking sheet lined with parchment paper. Top with pizza sauce and cover with mozzarella.

7. Bake for 20 to 25 minutes.

SIDE DISH IDEA

Orzo and Tomato Sauce

Cook 375 ml (1½ cups) orzo *al dente* in a pot of boiling, salted water. Drain. Bring 500 ml (2 cups) marinara sauce to boil in the same pot. Add the orzo and 45 ml (3 tbsp) chopped fresh basil. Season with salt and pepper. Reheat for 1 minute, stirring.

1 **Chicken flavoured instant noodles**
2 packages
(85 g each)

2 **Soy sauce**
60 ml (¼ cup)

3 **Cornstarch**
15 ml (1 tbsp)

4 **Pork**
675 g (1½ lb) loin chops, cut into strips

5 **Frozen stir-fry vegetable mix**
500 ml (2 cups)

OPTIONAL:
● **Fresh cilantro**
30 ml (2 tbsp) leaves

Pork and Ramen Stir-Fry

Prep time **15 minutes** • Cook time **6 minutes** • Serves **4**

Preparation

1. Whisk together the chicken stock powder included in the instant noodle packages with the soy sauce, corn starch and 250 ml (1 cup) of water.

2. Break the instant noodles into pieces.

3. Heat a little canola oil in a large pot over medium heat. Brown the pork strips for 1 minute on each side.

4. Add the mixed stir-fry vegetables and cook for 2 to 3 minutes, stirring.

5. Add the instant noodles and stock. Bring to a boil. Stir, and then cover and cook for 2 to 3 minutes.

6. Garnish with cilantro before serving, if desired.

 You can also use beef, vegetable or any other flavour of instant noodles!

PER SERVING	
Calories	336
Protein	46 g
Fat	16 g
Carbohydrates	35 g
Fibre	3 g
Iron	2 mg
Calcium	36 mg
Sodium	1,603 mg

SIDE DISH IDEA

Fried Wontons

Beat 1 egg yolk with a little water and brush over 16 wonton wrappers. Sprinkle with 15 ml (1 tbsp) sesame seeds. Cut the wrappers into triangles. Let sit for 5 minutes. Heat 125 ml (½ cup) canola oil in a deep pan over medium heat. Fry the wrappers for 15 seconds on each side.

1 **Pork**
4 pork chops, 2 cm
(¾ in) thick

2 **Onion soup mix**
1 package (28 g)

3 **Onion confit**
250 ml (1 cup)

4 **Gruyère**
grated
375 ml (1½ cups)

5 **Fresh parsley**
chopped
45 ml (3 tbsp)

Onion Soup
Pork Chop Gratin

Prep time **15 minutes** • Cook time **17 minutes** • Serves **4**

PER SERVING	
Calories	686
Protein	81 g
Fat	32 g
Carbohydrates	14 g
Fibre	1 g
Iron	2 mg
Calcium	491 mg
Sodium	1,105 mg

Preparation

1. Preheat the oven to 205°C (400°F).

2. Heat a little olive oil in an ovenproof skillet over medium heat. Brown the pork chops for 1 minute on each side. Transfer the pork chops to a plate.

3. In the same pan, mix the onion soup packets with 375 ml (1½ cups) of water. Bring to a boil and let simmer for 3 minutes over medium heat.

4. Return the pork chops to the pan. Spoon the onion confit onto the pork chops and then cover with Gruyère. Transfer to the oven and bake for 12 to 15 minutes.

5. Garnish with parsley before serving.

SIDE DISH IDEA

Baked Potatoes with Flavoured Sour Cream

Wrap 4 large potatoes individually in aluminum foil. Bake for 40 to 50 minutes at 205°C (400°F), until the potatoes are tender. In a bowl, mix 180 ml (¾ cup) sour cream with 15 ml (1 tbsp) salad seasoning and 60 ml (¼ cup) grated Parmesan. Remove the aluminum foil from the potatoes. Top the potatoes with the flavoured sour cream.

1 **Pork**
675 g (1½ lb)
tenderloin

2 **Fresh parsley**
chopped
60 ml (¼ cup)

3 **Fresh basil**
chopped
60 ml (¼ cup)

4 **Panko breadcrumbs**
250 ml (1 cup)

5 **Garlic and Fine Herbs cheese spread**
(like Boursin brand)
softened
1 package (150 g)

Herb-Crusted Pork Tenderloin

Prep time **15 minutes** • Cook time **20 minutes** • Serves **4**

PER SERVING	
Calories	419
Protein	41 g
Fat	21 g
Carbohydrates	14 g
Fibre	1 g
Iron	2 mg
Calcium	45 mg
Sodium	269 mg

Preparation

1. Preheat the oven to 205°C (400°F).

2. Trim the pork tenderloin by removing the silver skin.

3. Heat a little olive oil in a large frying pan over medium heat. Brown the pork tenderloin for 2 to 3 minutes on all sides. Remove from heat and let cool.

4. Mix the parsley, basil and panko breadcrumbs in a shallow bowl. Season with salt and pepper.

5. Brush the entire surface of the pork tenderloin with the cheese spread. Coat the tenderloin with the breadcrumb mixture.

6. Place the tenderloin on a baking sheet lined with parchment paper. Drizzle with olive oil. Bake for 18 to 20 minutes.

7. Remove the tenderloin from the oven and transfer to a plate. Cover loosely with aluminum foil. Let rest for 5 minutes before slicing.

You can replace the Boursin type cheese spread with herb-flavoured cream cheese or goat cheese.

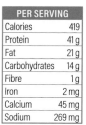

SIDE DISH IDEA

Parmesan Brussels Sprouts

Cut 450 g (1 lb) Brussels sprouts in half. In a bowl, mix the Brussels sprouts with 30 ml (2 tbsp) olive oil, 60 ml (¼ cup) chopped shallots, 2 minced cloves garlic and 125 ml (½ cup) grated Parmesan. Season with salt and pepper. Spread the mixture onto a baking sheet lined with parchment paper. Bake for 18 to 20 minutes at 205°C (400°F), until the Brussels sprouts are tender.

1 **8 Italian sausages**
sliced into rounds

2 **Cajun spices**
store-bought
30 ml (2 tbsp)

3 **3 pepper halves**
various colours
chopped

4 **Long grain
white rice**
250 ml (1 cup)

5 **Condensed tomato
soup**
1 can (284 ml)

ALSO NEEDED:
● **1 onion**
chopped

Cajun Sausage and Rice

Prep time **15 minutes** • Cook time **22 minutes** • Serves **4**

PER SERVING	
Calories	690
Protein	28 g
Fat	31 g
Carbohydrates	74 g
Fibre	3 g
Iron	3 mg
Calcium	56 mg
Sodium	1,696 mg

Preparation

1. Preheat the oven to 205°C (400°F).

2. Heat a little olive oil in an ovenproof skillet over medium heat. Brown the sausages for 1 minute on each side.

3. Add the onion, Cajun spices, peppers, rice, tomato soup and 430 ml (1¾ cups) of water. Season with salt and pepper, and stir. Bring to a boil, and then cover and bake for 20 to 25 minutes, until the liquid is completely absorbed.

HOMEMADE VERSION

Cajun Spices

Mix 15 ml (1 tbsp) sweet smoked paprika with 15 ml (1 tbsp) onion powder, 15 ml (1 tbsp) garlic powder, 10 ml (2 tsp) dried oregano, 5 ml (1 tsp) dried thyme and 1.25 ml (¼ tsp) cayenne pepper.

Asian-Style Pork Tenderloin

Prep time **15 minutes** • Cook time **21 minutes** • Serves **4**

PER SERVING	
Calories	380
Protein	39 g
Fat	9 g
Carbohydrates	32 g
Fibre	0 g
Iron	2 mg
Calcium	20 mg
Sodium	1,320 mg

Preparation

1. Preheat the oven to 205°C (400°F).

2. Trim the pork tenderloin by removing the silver skin.

3. Heat a little oil in an ovenproof skillet over medium heat. Brown the pork tenderloin for 2 to 3 minutes on each side.

4. Add the ginger and garlic. Cook for 1 minute.

5. Add the sweet chili sauce, soy sauce, honey, and sriracha if desired. Cover, and then transfer to the oven and bake for 18 to 20 minutes.

6. Remove the skillet from the oven and transfer the tenderloin to a plate. Cover loosely with aluminum foil. Let rest for 5 minutes before slicing.

7. Serve the tenderloin with the remaining sauce from the skillet.

SIDE DISH IDEA

Vegetable Rice

Heat 15 ml (1 tbsp) olive oil in a pot over medium heat. Cook 250 ml (1 cup) frozen diced vegetable mix for 2 to 3 minutes. Add 250 ml (1 cup) basmati rice, rinsed and drained. Stir. Pour in 500 ml (2 cups) chicken stock. Bring to a boil, and then cover and let simmer over low heat for 18 to 20 minutes, until the liquid is completely absorbed.

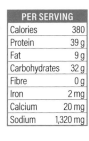

1 **Pork**
675 g (1½ lb)
tenderloin

2 **Ginger**
chopped
15 ml (1 tbsp)

3 **Sweet chili sauce**
180 ml (¾ cup)

4 **Soy sauce**
60 ml (¼ cup)

5 **Honey**
30 ml (2 tbsp)

ALSO NEEDED:
● **Garlic**
minced
15 ml (1 tbsp)

OPTIONAL:
● **Sriracha**
5 ml (1 tsp)

1 **Barbecue sauce**
125 ml (½ cup)

2 **Apple juice**
250 ml (1 cup)

3 **1 onion**
chopped

4 **Pork seasoning**
15 ml (1 tbsp)

5 **Pork**
4 pork chops

Barbecue Pork Chops

Prep time **15 minutes** • Cook time **10 minutes** • Serves **4**

PER SERVING	
Calories	394
Protein	48 g
Fat	9 g
Carbohydrates	26 g
Fibre	1 g
Iron	2 mg
Calcium	29 mg
Sodium	957 mg

Preparation

1. Preheat the oven to 180°C (350°F).

2. Mix the barbecue sauce, apple juice, onion and pork seasoning in a bowl.

3. Heat a little olive oil in an ovenproof skillet over medium heat. Brown the pork chops for 1 minute on each side.

4. Add the sauce to the skillet. Transfer to the oven and bake for 8 to 10 minutes.

SIDE DISH IDEA

Apple Coleslaw

In a salad bowl, mix 60 ml (¼ cup) mayonnaise with 60 ml (¼ cup) orange juice, 30 ml (2 tbsp) fresh lemon juice, 15 ml (1 tbsp) sugar and 60 ml (¼ cup) chopped fresh parsley. Season with salt and pepper. Add 625 ml (2½ cups) green cabbage, finely chopped, and 1 large carrot and 2 green apples, cut into thin julienne strips. Stir.

1 **4 potatoes**
peeled and cubed

2 **California blend
frozen vegetables**
750 ml (3 cups)

3 **Four cheese
Alfredo sauce**
625 ml (2½ cups)

4 **Ham**
cubed
450 g (1 lb)

5 **Swiss cheese**
grated
375 ml (1½ cups)

Ham and Vegetable Gratin

Prep time **15 minutes** • Cook time **30 minutes** • Serves **4**

PER SERVING	
Calories	679
Protein	42 g
Fat	38 g
Carbohydrates	46 g
Fibre	7 g
Fer	2 mg
Calcium	805 mg
Sodium	2,099 mg

Preparation

1. Preheat the oven to 205°C (400°F).

2. Place the potato cubes in a pot and cover with cold water. Season with salt. Bring to a boil, and then cover and cook for 10 minutes. About 5 minutes before the potatoes are cooked, add the vegetable blend to the pot. Drain.

3. In the same pot, bring the Alfredo sauce to a boil.

4. Add the potatoes, vegetables and ham to the Alfredo sauce. Season with pepper and stir.

5. Grease a 23 cm (9 in) baking dish, and then transfer the prepared ingredients into it. Cover with Swiss cheese. Bake for 20 to 25 minutes.

⇨ Check out our recipe for a homemade California vegetable blend on page 25.

SIDE DISH IDEA

Cucumber and Radish Salad

In a salad bowl, mix 1 head of Boston lettuce, chopped, with 1 diced English cucumber, 8 quartered radishes, 1 small red onion, sliced, and 125 ml (½ cup) maple mustard dressing.

BEEF & VEAL

Beef and veal recipes that are simple,
tasty, and require just 5 ingredients—can
it be done? Oh yes! We've got the proof
right here. Your guests will be wowed
when you serve up beef Stroganoff or
veal Milanese. It's up to you whether
or not to let them in on the secret!

1 **Medium ground beef**
450 g (1 lb)

2 **Rice**
cooked
500 ml (2 cups)

3 **Marinara sauce**
250 ml (1 cup)

4 **4 peppers**
various colours

5 **Italian shredded cheese blend**
375 ml (1½ cups)

ALSO NEEDED:
● **1 onion**
chopped

Stuffed Peppers

Prep time **15 minutes** • Cook time **36 minutes** • Serves **4**

PER SERVING	
Calories	641
Protein	37 g
Fat	35 g
Carbohydrates	45 g
Fibre	6 g
Iron	3 mg
Calcium	366 mg
Sodium	431 mg

Preparation

1. Preheat the oven to 205°C (400°F).

2. Heat a little olive oil in a large frying pan over medium heat. Cook the ground beef for 5 to 7 minutes, breaking up the meat with a wooden spoon, until it is no longer pink.

3. Add the onion and cook for 1 minute, stirring.

4. Stir in the cooked rice and marinara sauce. Bring to a boil.

5. Slice off the tops of the peppers and remove the white membrane and seeds.

6. Stuff the peppers with the beef mixture. Cover with cheese.

7. Place the stuffed peppers on a baking dish lined with parchment paper. Bake for 30 to 35 minutes.

⇨ Check out our recipe for homemade marinara sauce on page 246!

SIDE DISH IDEA

Creamy Salad

In a salad bowl, mix 125 ml (½ cup) 15% country-style cream with 3 green onions, chopped. Season with salt and pepper. Add 1 head of green curly leaf lettuce, chopped, and toss.

1 **Egg noodles**
500 ml (2 cups)

2 **Beef**
450 g (1 lb) sirloin
steak, cut into strips
or pieces

3 **Mushrooms**
sliced
1 container (227 g)

4 **Gravy**
500 ml (2 cups)

5 **Sour cream (14%)**
125 ml (½ cup)

OPTIONAL:
● **Fresh parsley**
chopped
60 ml (¼ cup)

Beef Stroganoff Over Egg Noodles

Prep time **15 minutes** • Cook time **10 minutes** • Serves **4**

PER SERVING	
Calories	356
Protein	33 g
Fat	13 g
Carbohydrates	25 g
Fibre	1 g
Iron	4 mg
Calcium	63 mg
Sodium	847 mg

Preparation

1. Cook the pasta *al dente* in a pot of boiling salted water. Drain.

2. Heat a little olive oil in a frying pan over medium heat. Cook the beef strips for 1 minute on each side.

3. Add the mushrooms to the pan and cook for 2 minutes.

4. Add the gravy and sour cream. Bring to a boil, and let simmer for 3 to 4 minutes over medium-low heat.

5. Divide the pasta onto plates. Top each serving with beef Stroganoff, and parsley if desired.

 You can replace the egg noodles with long pasta or white rice!

SIDE DISH IDEA

Summer Salad

In a salad bowl, mix 125 ml (½ cup) Tuscan Italian dressing with 1 head of romaine lettuce, chopped, 3 half peppers of various colours, sliced, and 375 ml (1½ cups) seasoned salad croutons.

1 **Lean ground beef**
600 g (1⅓ lb)

2 **2 red peppers**
diced

3 **Mild salsa**
500 ml (2 cups)

4 **Tortillas**
5 large

5 **Tex-Mex shredded
cheese blend**
625 ml (2½ cups)

Layered Taco Casserole

Prep time **15 minutes** • Cook time **36 minutes** • Serves **4**

PER SERVING	
Calories	778
Protein	49 g
Fat	44 g
Carbohydrates	42 g
Fibre	5 g
Iron	5 mg
Calcium	165 mg
Sodium	1,286 mg

Preparation

1. Preheat the oven to 190°C (375°F).

2. Heat a little olive oil in a frying pan over medium heat. Cook the ground beef for 5 to 7 minutes, breaking up the meat with a wooden spoon, until it is no longer pink.

3. Add the red peppers to the pan and cook for 1 minute.

4. Stir in the salsa. Bring to a boil, then let simmer for 10 to 12 minutes over low heat.

5. Stack two tortillas in a lightly greased ovenproof skillet. Spread with a third of the beef mixture and a quarter of the cheese. Top with one tortilla. Repeat these steps for two more layers. Cover with the remaining cheese. Bake for 20 to 25 minutes.

SIDE DISH IDEA

Avocado Salsa

In a bowl, mix 30 ml (2 tbsp) olive oil with 30 ml (2 tbsp) chopped fresh cilantro, 1 small red onion, diced, 30 ml (2 tbsp) fresh lime juice, 2 Italian tomatoes, seeded, and 2 avocados, diced. Season with salt and pepper.

120

1 **Frozen chopped spinach**
thawed and fully drained
1 bag (500 g)

2 **Ricotta cheese**
250 g (about ½ lb)

3 **Veal**
8 cutlets, 80 g
(about 2¾ oz) each

4 **Prosciutto**
8 slices

5 **Marinara sauce**
500 ml (2 cups)

Prosciutto, Spinach and Ricotta Veal Rolls

Prep time **15 minutes** • Cook time **11 minutes** • Serves **4**

PER SERVING	
Calories	550
Protein	66 g
Fat	23 g
Carbohydrates	18 g
Fibre	8 g
Iron	6 mg
Calcium	382 mg
Sodium	1,197 mg

Preparation

1. Mix the spinach and ricotta in a bowl. Season with salt and pepper.

2. Place a slice of prosciutto on each cutlet. Spoon some of the spinach mixture onto the base of each cutlet. Roll up the cutlets tightly and secure them with toothpicks.

3. Heat a little olive oil in a frying pan over medium heat. Sear the roulades for 1 to 2 minutes on all sides.

4. Pour the marinara sauce into the pan and bring to a boil. Cover and let simmer for 10 to 12 minutes over low heat.

 You can replace the veal with slices of inside round steak or pork cutlets!

SIDE DISH IDEA

Garlic and Basil Rice

Melt 15 ml (1 tbsp) butter in a pot over medium heat. Cook 15 ml (1 tbsp) minced garlic and 250 ml (1 cup) basmati rice, rinsed and drained, for 30 seconds. Pour in 500 ml (2 cups) vegetable stock and bring to a boil. Cover and cook for 18 to 20 minutes, until the liquid is completely absorbed. Add 45 ml (3 tbsp) chopped fresh basil and stir.

1 **Lean ground beef**
450 g (1 lb)

2 **4 potatoes**
peeled and cubed

3 **2 carrots**
sliced into rounds

Ground Beef and Veggie Skillet

Prep time **15 minutes** • Cook time **21 minutes** • Serves **4**

PER SERVING	
Calories	487
Protéines	30 g
Matières grasses	19 g
Glucides	47 g
Fibres	7 g
Fer	5 mg
Calcium	75 mg
Sodium	936 mg

Preparation

1. Heat a little olive oil in a large frying pan over medium heat. Cook the ground beef for 5 to 7 minutes, breaking up the meat with a wooden spoon, until it is no longer pink.

2. Add the onions and cook for 1 minute.

3. Add the potatoes and carrots. Pour in the sauce and 180 ml (¾ cup) of water. Season with salt and pepper, and stir. Bring to a boil, and then cover and cook for 10 to 13 minutes over medium-low heat.

4. Add the green peas, and parsley if desired. Stir and cook for another 5 minutes.

A LITTLE EXTRA

Tomato Chutney

Dice 1 onion and 3 Italian tomatoes, seeded. In a small pot, mix 15 ml (1 tbsp) cider vinegar with 15 ml (1 tbsp) brown sugar and 5 ml (1 tsp) minced garlic. Add the tomatoes and onion. Stir. Bring to a boil and then let simmer for 3 to 4 minutes over medium heat.

4 **Gravy**
500 ml (2 cups)

ALSO NEEDED:
• **2 onions**
chopped

OPTIONAL:
• **Fresh parsley**
chopped
45 ml (3 tbsp)

5 **Green peas**
500 ml (2 cups)

1 **Beef**
675 g (1½ lb)
sirloin steak,
cut into strips

2 **Ginger**
chopped
15 ml (1 tbsp)

3 **½ head broccoli**
cut into small
florets

4 **Thick teriyaki sauce**
store-bought
80 ml (⅓ cup)

5 **Beef stock**
80 ml (⅓ cup)

ALSO NEEDED:
- **1 onion**
  thinly sliced
- **Garlic**
  minced
  15 ml (1 tbsp)

Teriyaki Beef and Broccoli Stir-Fry

Prep time **15 minutes** • Cook time **7 minutes** • Serves **4**

PER SERVING	
Calories	299
Protein	39 g
Fat	10 g
Carbohydrates	11 g
Fibre	1 g
Iron	4 mg
Calcium	25 mg
Sodium	521 mg

Preparation

1. Heat a little canola oil in a frying pan over medium heat. Cook the beef strips for 1 minute on each side. Set aside on a plate.

2. In the same pan, cook the onion, garlic and ginger for 1 minute, stirring.

3. Add the broccoli and cook for 2 minutes.

4. Add the beef, teriyaki sauce and stock. Bring to a boil and let simmer for 2 minutes.

HOMEMADE VERSION

Teriyaki Sauce

In a pot, mix 60 ml (¼ cup) soy sauce with 45 ml (3 tbsp) mirin, 80 ml (⅓ cup) beef stock, 10 ml (2 tsp) minced garlic, 7.5 ml (1½ tsp) cornstarch and 30 ml (2 tbsp) brown sugar. Bring to a boil, whisking.

1 **Medium ground beef**
450 g (1 lb)

2 **Frozen mixed vegetables**
thawed and drained
500 ml (2 cups)

3 **Alfredo sauce**
625 ml (2½ cups)

4 **4 small sweet potatoes**
peeled and sliced

5 **Swiss cheese**
grated
375 ml (1½ cups)

ALSO NEEDED:
- **1 onion**
  chopped

Ground Beef and Sweet Potato Casserole

Prep time **15 minutes** • Cook time **32 minutes** • Serves **4**

PER SERVING	
Calories	834
Protein	45 g
Fat	54 g
Carbohydrates	52 g
Fibre	8 g
Iron	4 mg
Calcium	682 mg
Sodium	903 mg

Preparation

1. Preheat the oven to 205°C (400°F).

2. Heat a little olive oil in a pot over medium heat. Cook the ground beef for 5 to 7 minutes, breaking up the meat with a wooden spoon, until it is no longer pink.

3. Add the onion and mixed vegetables. Cook for 2 to 3 minutes.

4. Add the Alfredo sauce. Stir and bring to a boil.

5. Pour the mixture into a 33 cm x 23 cm (13 in x 9 in) baking dish. Cover with sweet potato slices, and then cheese. Bake for 25 to 30 minutes.

 You can replace the sweet potatoes with regular potatoes!

SIDE DISH IDEA

Iceberg Coleslaw

In a salad bowl, mix 60 ml (¼ cup) sour cream with 45 ml (3 tbsp) mayonnaise, 30 ml (2 tbsp) cider vinegar, 15 ml (1 tbsp) sugar and 60 ml (¼ cup) chopped fresh parsley. Season with salt and pepper. Add 1 head of iceberg lettuce, finely chopped, and 1 shredded carrot. Stir.

1 **Medium ground beef**
450 g (1 lb)

2 **White rice**
cooked
125 ml (½ cup)

3 **1 onion**
chopped

4 **Worcestershire sauce**
15 ml (1 tbsp)

5 **Tomato sauce**
500 ml (2 cups)

OPTIONAL:
● **Fresh parsley**
chopped
60 ml (¼ cup)

Beef and Rice Porcupine Meatballs

Prep time **15 minutes** • Cook time **12 minutes** • Serves **4**

PER SERVING	
Calories	385
Protein	25 g
Fat	22 g
Carbohydrates	22 g
Fibre	4 g
Iron	3 mg
Calcium	36 mg
Sodium	583 mg

Preparation

1. In a bowl, combine the ground beef with the cooked rice, onion, Worcestershire sauce, and parsley if desired. Season with salt and pepper.

2. Form 20 meatballs, using about 30 ml (2 tbsp) of the preparation for each one.

3. Heat a little olive oil in a frying pan over medium heat. Brown the meatballs for 2 to 3 minutes on all sides.

4. Add the tomato sauce to the pan and bring to a boil. Let simmer for 10 to 12 minutes, until the meatballs are no longer pink in the centre.

SIDE DISH IDEA

Potato and Parsnip Puree

Peel and cube 3 potatoes and 3 parsnips. Place the potatoes and parsnips in a pot. Cover the potatoes with cold salted water. Bring to a boil, and then cover and cook for 20 to 25 minutes, until tender. Drain. Puree with 60 ml (¼ cups) warm 15% cooking cream, 80 ml (⅓ cup) grated Parmesan and 30 ml (2 tbsp) chopped fresh chives. Season with salt and pepper.

1 **Flour**
125 ml (½ cup)

2 **2 eggs**

3 **Italian-style breadcrumbs**
250 ml (1 cup)

4 **Veal**
8 small cutlets, 60 g (about 2¼ oz) each

5 **1 lemon**
cut into wedges

Veal Milanese

Prep time **15 minutes** • Cook time **4 minutes** • Serves **4**

PER SERVING	
Calories	408
Protein	36 g
Fat	13 g
Carbohydrates	37 g
Fibre	3 g
Iron	5 mg
Calcium	93 mg
Sodium	504 mg

Preparation

1. Set out three shallow bowls. Put the flour in the first. Beat the eggs in the second. Pour the breadcrumbs into the third.

2. Coat the cutlets in flour and shake to remove the excess. Dip the cutlets in the beaten eggs, and then coat with the breadcrumbs.

3. Heat a little canola oil in a frying pan over medium heat. Cook the cutlets for 2 minutes on each side.

4. Serve the cutlets with the lemon wedges.

 You can replace the veal with pork or chicken cutlets!

SIDE DISH IDEA

Arugula and Parmesan Pasta Salad

Cook 500 ml (2 cups) gemelli pasta *al dente* in a pot of boiling salted water. Drain and rinse under cold water. Drain again. In a salad bowl, mix 125 ml (½ cup) mayonnaise with 80 ml (⅓ cup) plain yogurt and 15 ml (1 tbsp) salad seasoning. Add the pasta, 125 ml (½ cup) grated Parmesan and 500 ml (2 cups) arugula. Stir.

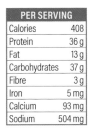

1 **Medium
ground beef**
450 g (1 lb)

2 **Frozen diced
vegetable mix**
thawed
and drained
750 ml (3 cups)

3 **Chili seasoning**
store-bought
1 packet (24 g)

4 **Crushed tomatoes**
1 can (796 ml)

5 **Kidney beans**
rinsed and drained
1 can (540 ml)

OPTIONAL:
● **Corn chips**
to taste

Classic Chili

Prep time **15 minutes** • Cook time **28 minutes** • Serves **4**

PER SERVING	
Calories	524
Protein	34 g
Fat	23 g
Carbohydrates	47 g
Fibre	14 g
Iron	8 mg
Calcium	139 mg
Sodium	984 mg

Preparation

1. Heat a little canola oil in a large pot over medium heat. Cook the ground beef for 5 to 7 minutes, breaking up the meat with a wooden spoon, until it is no longer pink.

2. Add the mixed vegetables and chili seasoning. Continue cooking for 3 to 4 minutes, stirring occasionally.

3. Add the crushed tomatoes and bring to a boil over low heat. Let simmer for 15 to 20 minutes.

4. Add the kidney beans and cook for another 5 minutes. Season with salt and pepper.

5. Serve the chili with corn chips if desired.

 You can also serve your chili with cheese, sour cream and green onions!

HOMEMADE VERSION
Chili Seasoning

Mix 15 ml (1 tbsp) paprika with 10 ml (2 tsp) chili powder, 5 ml (1 tsp) sugar, 5 ml (1 tsp) salt, 2.5 ml (½ tsp) cumin, 2.5 ml (½ tsp) onion powder, 2.5 ml (½ tsp) garlic powder and 1.25 ml (¼ tsp) cayenne pepper.

1 **3 oranges**

2 **Beef**
450 g (1 lb) sirloin
steak, cut into strips

3 **Ginger**
minced
15 ml (1 tbsp)

4 **Molasses**
15 ml (1 tbsp)

5 **Teriyaki
marinade sauce**
125 ml (½ cup)

Orange Beef

Prep time **15 minutes** • Cook time **7 minutes** • Serves **4**

PER SERVING	
Calories	280
Protein	29 g
Fat	8 g
Carbohydrates	21 g
Fibre	2 g
Iron	3 mg
Calcium	63 mg
Sodium	1,342 mg

Preparation

1. Supreme the oranges by using a knife to cut off the rind and then slicing along either side of the membranes. Squeeze the membranes over a small bowl to collect the juice. Set aside the supremed orange wedges.

2. Heat a little canola oil in a frying pan over medium heat. Cook the beef strips for 1 minute on each side.

3. Add the ginger and garlic. Cook for 1 minute.

4. Add the orange juice, molasses and teriyaki sauce. Bring to a boil and then let simmer for 3 to 4 minutes.

5. Add the orange wedges and stir. Heat for 1 minute.

6. Garnish with green onion before serving if desired.

SIDE DISH IDEA

Sesame Baby Bok-Choy

Heat 15 ml (1 tbsp) sesame oil (untoasted) in a frying pan over medium heat. Cook 1 onion, chopped, and 2 cloves of garlic, minced, for 1 minute. Add 20 heads of baby bok-choy. Season with salt and pepper. Cook for 3 to 4 minutes, stirring a few times. Garnish with 15 ml (1 tbsp) sesame seeds.

ALSO NEEDED:
● **Garlic**
minced
15 ml (1 tbsp)

OPTIONAL:
● **3 green onions**
chopped

1 **1 spaghetti squash**

2 **Lean ground beef** 450 g (1 lb)

3 **Frozen diced vegetable mix** 500 ml (2 cups)

4 **Tomato sauce** 500 ml (2 cups)

5 **Mozzarella** shredded 500 ml (2 cups)

Bolognese Spaghetti Squash

Prep time **15 minutes** • Cook time **55 minutes** • Serves **4**

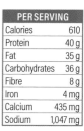

PER SERVING	
Calories	610
Protein	40 g
Fat	35 g
Carbohydrates	36 g
Fibre	8 g
Iron	4 mg
Calcium	435 mg
Sodium	1,047 mg

Preparation

1. Preheat the oven to 205°C (400°F).

2. Cut the spaghetti squash in half lengthwise. Remove the seeds and stringy flesh.

3. Place the squash halves on a baking sheet lined with parchment paper, flesh side up. Drizzle with olive oil. Season with salt and pepper.

4. Bake for 35 to 40 minutes, until the flesh of the squash shreds easily with a fork.

5. While the squash is cooking, heat a little olive oil in a pot over medium heat. Cook the ground beef for 5 to 7 minutes, breaking the meat up with a wooden spoon, until it is no longer pink.

6. Add the vegetable mix and cook for 2 to 3 minutes.

7. Pour in the tomato sauce and bring to a boil. Cook for 15 to 18 minutes over medium-low heat, until the bolognese sauce reaches the desired consistency.

8. Remove the squash halves from the oven and shred the flesh with a fork, taking care not to cut the skin.

9. Top the squash halves with bolognese sauce and mozzarella. Bake for 20 to 25 minutes.

⇨ Check out our recipe for a homemade frozen vegetable mix for spaghetti on page 25.

SIDE DISH IDEA

Panzanella

In a salad bowl, mix 80 ml (⅓ cup) olive oil with 15 ml (1 tbsp) white balsamic vinegar and 45 ml (3 tbsp) chopped fresh basil. Season with salt and pepper. Add 375 ml (1½ cups) seasoned salad croutons, 1 small red onion, chopped, half of an English cucumber, chopped, and 12 cherry tomatoes, halved. Stir.

1 **Beef**
4 sirloin steaks,
180 g (about ⅓ lb)
each

2 **1 onion**
chopped

3 **1 red pepper**
chopped

4 **Diced tomatoes**
1 can (540 ml)

5 **Paprika**
15 ml (1 tbsp)

Skillet Swiss Steak

Prep time **15 minutes** • Cook time **11 minutes** • Serves **4**

PER SERVING	
Calories	329
Protein	43 g
Fat	11 g
Carbohydrates	14 g
Fibre	2 g
Iron	6 mg
Calcium	74 mg
Sodium	316 mg

Preparation

1. Heat a little olive oil in a frying pan over medium heat.
Cook the steaks for 1 minute on each side. Set aside on a plate.

2. Place the onion and pepper in the pan. Cook for 2 minutes.

3. Add the diced tomatoes and paprika. Season with salt and pepper,
and stir. Bring to a boil and then let simmer for 5 minutes over
medium-low heat.

4. Add the steaks and cook for another 2 to 3 minutes.

SIDE DISH IDEA

Pan-Fried Gnocchi and Fresh Herbs

Cook 350 g (about ¾ lb) of fresh gnocchi
in a pot of boiling salted water according to the instructions on the package.
Drain. Melt 30 ml (2 tbsp) butter in a
frying pan over medium heat. Brown the
gnocchi for 2 to 3 minutes. Add 30 ml (2 tbsp)
chopped fresh parsley, 30 ml (2 tbsp) chopped fresh
basil and 80 ml (⅓ cup) grated Parmesan.
Season with salt and pepper, and stir.

1 **Lean ground beef**
450 g (1 lb)

2 **Hulled barley**
180 ml (¾ cup)

3 **Beef stock**
1 litre (4 cups)

4 **Diced tomatoes
with Italian spices**
1 can (796 ml)

5 **Frozen vegetables
for soup**
500 ml (2 cups)

Beef and Barley Soup

Prep time **15 minutes** • Cook time **45 minutes** • Serves **4**

PER SERVING	
Calories	465
Protein	32 g
Fat	20 g
Carbohydrates	28 g
Fibre	6 g
Iron	6 mg
Calcium	153 mg
Sodium	1,190 mg

Preparation

1. Heat a little olive oil in a pot over medium heat. Cook the ground beef for 5 to 7 minutes, breaking up the meat with a wooden spoon, until it is no longer pink. Drain the excess fat from the pot.

2. Add the barley, stock and diced tomatoes to the pot. Season with salt and pepper, and stir. Bring to a boil and then let simmer for 20 minutes over low heat.

3. Add the mixed vegetables and cook for another 20 to 25 minutes.

⇨ **Check out our recipe for homemade frozen vegetable mix for soup on page 25.**

SIDE DISH IDEA

Olive Oil and Salt Croutons

Cut half of a baguette into 12 slices. Place the bread slices on a baking sheet lined with parchment paper. Drizzle with 30 ml (2 tbsp) olive oil and sprinkle with 5 ml (1 tsp) *fleur de sel*. Bake for 8 to 10 minutes at 190°C (375°F).

1 **Medium ground beef**
450 g (1 lb)

2 **15 saltine crackers**
crushed into breadcrumbs

3 **1 egg**

4 **Barbecue sauce**
180 ml (¾ cup)

5 **Yellow cheddar**
shredded
375 ml (1½ cups)

ALSO NEEDED:
● **1 onion**
chopped

Mini Cheesy Barbecue Meatloaves

Prep time **15 minutes** • Cook time **25 minutes** • Serves **4**

PER SERVING	
Calories	632
Protein	35 g
Fat	39 g
Carbohydrates	33 g
Fibre	1 g
Iron	4 mg
Calcium	355 mg
Sodium	885 mg

Preparation

1. Preheat the oven to 205°C (400°F).

2. In a bowl, mix the ground beef with the saltine cracker crumbs, egg, onion, half of the barbecue sauce and half of the cheddar. Season with salt and pepper.

3. Grease 8 cups of a muffin tin and evenly distribute the mixture among them. Top with the remaining barbecue sauce and cheddar.

4. Bake for 25 to 30 minutes, until the mini meatloaves are no longer pink in the centre.

 You can replace the saltine crackers with 125 ml (½ cup) of breadcrumbs or other crackers crushed into breadcrumbs!

SIDE DISH IDEA
Roasted Cauliflower and Sweet Potatoes

Cut half of a head of cauliflower into florets, 1 onion into wedges and 2 sweet potatoes into cubes. In a bowl, mix the vegetables with 15 ml (1 tbsp) chopped fresh thyme. Season with salt and pepper, and stir. Spread the vegetables over a baking sheet lined with parchment paper. Bake for 30 to 35 minutes at 205°C (400°F).

1 **3 pepper halves**
various colours
sliced

2 **Garlic**
minced
15 ml (1 tbsp)

3 **Maple syrup**
80 ml (⅓ cup)

4 **Beef**
8 slices of inside
round steak

5 **Balsamic vinegar**
30 ml (2 tbsp)

Balsamic Steak Rolls

Prep time **15 minutes** • Cook time **8 minutes** • Serves **4**

PER SERVING	
Calories	269
Protein	28 g
Fat	6 g
Carbohydrates	24 g
Fibre	1 g
Iron	3 mg
Calcium	47 mg
Sodium	80 mg

Preparation

1. Heat a little olive oil in a frying pan over medium heat. Cook the peppers and garlic for 2 to 3 minutes.

2. Pour in a third of the maple syrup. Season with salt and pepper. Cook for 2 minutes. Remove from heat and let cool.

3. Evenly spread the pepper mixture onto the base of each steak slice. Roll the slices up tightly and secure with a toothpick.

4. Heat a little olive oil in the same frying pan over medium heat. Sear the rolls for 2 to 3 minutes on each side.

5. Pour the balsamic vinegar and remaining maple syrup into the pan. Bring to a boil and cook for 2 to 3 minutes.

SIDE DISH IDEA

Zucchini and Cheese Rice

Melt 30 ml (2 tbsp) butter in a pot over medium heat. Cook 125 ml (½ cup) chopped shallots and 15 ml (1 tbsp) minced garlic for 1 minute. Add 250 ml (1 cup) basmati rice, rinsed and drained, and 500 ml (2 cups) chicken stock. Season with salt and pepper, and stir. Bring to a boil, then cover and let simmer for 18 to 20 minutes, until the liquid is completely absorbed. Add 1 zucchini, grated, and 250 ml (1 cup) sharp Cheddar, shredded. Stir.

1 **Medium ground beef**
450 g (1 lb)

2 **Diced tomatoes**
1 can (540 ml)

3 **Tomato sauce with herbs**
375 ml (1½ cups)

4 **½ head green cabbage**
chopped

5 **Basmati rice**
rinsed and drained
180 ml (¾ cup)

ALSO NEEDED:
- **1 onion**
  chopped

Skillet Cabbage Roll

Prep time **15 minutes** • Cook time **24 minutes** • Serves **4**

PER SERVING	
Calories	530
Protein	30 g
Fat	22 g
Carbohydrates	54 g
Fibre	7 g
Iron	9 mg
Calcium	138 mg
Sodium	710 mg

Preparation

1. Heat a little olive oil in a pot over medium heat. Cook the ground beef for 5 to 7 minutes, breaking up the meat with a wooden spoon, until it is no longer pink.

2. Add the onion and cook for 1 minute.

3. Add the diced tomatoes and tomato sauce. Bring to a boil.

4. Add the cabbage. Season with salt and pepper, and stir. Let simmer for 18 to 20 minutes over low heat.

5. While the cabbage is cooking, place the rice in a pot with 375 ml (1½ cups) of water. Season with salt. Bring to a boil, then cover and let simmer for 18 to 20 minutes, until the liquid is completely absorbed.

6. Divide the rice onto plates. Top with the prepared beef.

💡 If you prefer, you can also mix the rice with the prepared beef directly in the pot before serving.

SIDE DISH IDEA

Roasted Zucchini Sticks

In a bowl, mix four small zucchinis cut into sticks with 10 ml (2 tsp) olive oil, 15 ml (1 tbsp) Italian seasoning and 60 ml (¼ cup) grated Parmesan. Season with salt and pepper. Spread the zucchini sticks on a baking sheet lined with parchment paper. Bake for 12 to 15 minutes at 220°C (425°F), turning them over at the halfway point.

1 **Lean ground beef**
450 g (1 lb)

2 **1 onion**
chopped

3 **Ginger**
minced
15 ml (1 tbsp)

4 **Brown sugar**
30 ml (2 tbsp)

5 **Soy sauce**
60 ml (¼ cup)

ALSO NEEDED:
● **Garlic**
minced
15 ml (1 tbsp)

OPTIONAL:
● **Pepper flakes**
1.25 ml (¼ tsp)

Korean Ground Beef

Prep time **15 minutes** • Cook time **9 minutes** • Serves **4**

Preparation

1. Heat a little canola oil in a frying pan over medium heat. Cook the ground beef for 5 to 7 minutes, breaking up the meat with a wooden spoon, until it is no longer pink.

2. Add the onion, ginger, brown sugar, soy sauce, garlic, and pepper flakes if desired, to the pan. Stir. Cook for 4 to 5 minutes over medium-low heat.

PER SERVING	
Calories	311
Protein	24 g
Fat	19 g
Carbohydrates	10 g
Fibre	1 g
Iron	2 mg
Calcium	35 mg
Sodium	963 mg

SIDE DISH IDEA

Sesame Rice

Heat 15 ml (1 tbsp) canola oil in a pot over medium heat. Cook 125 ml (½ cup) chopped shallots with 15 ml (1 tbsp) lime zest for 1 minute. Add 250 ml (1 cup) basmati rice, rinsed and drained, 500 ml (2 cups) chicken stock and 15 ml (1 tbsp) tahini (sesame paste). Season with salt and pepper. Bring to a boil, and then cover and let simmer for 18 to 20 minutes, until the liquid is completely absorbed.

1 Medium
ground beef
450 g (1 lb)

2 **Frozen diced**
vegetable mix
500 ml (2 cups)

3 **Condensed**
tomato soup
1 can (284 ml)

4 **Basmati rice**
cooked
500 ml (2 cups)

5 **Mozzarella**
shredded
375 ml (1½ cups)

ALSO NEEDED:
● **Beef stock**
250 ml (1 cup)

Ground Beef, Tomato and Rice au Gratin

Prep time **15 minutes** • Cook time **25 minutes** • Serves **4**

PER SERVING	
Calories	615
Protein	36 g
Fat	33 g
Carbohydrates	41 g
Fibre	3 g
Iron	3 mg
Calcium	310 mg
Sodium	1,023 mg

Preparation

1. Preheat the oven to 205°C (400°F).

2. Heat a little olive oil in a large frying pan over medium heat. Cook the ground beef with the vegetable mix for 5 to 7 minutes, breaking up the meat with a wooden spoon, until it is no longer pink.

3. Add the tomato soup and beef stock to the pan. Season with salt and pepper, and stir. Bring to a boil over medium heat.

4. Add the cooked rice and stir.

5. Pour the mixture into a 23 cm (9 in) baking dish. Cover with mozzarella. Bake for 8 to 10 minutes, until the cheese is melted.

6. Broil for 2 to 3 minutes.

⇨ Check out our recipe for homemade frozen diced vegetable mix on page 25.

SIDE DISH IDEA

Almond and Plum Spring Salad

In a salad bowl, mix 45 ml (3 tbsp) olive oil with 30 ml (2 tbsp) cider vinegar and 15 ml (1 tbsp) maple syrup. Season with salt and pepper. Add 1 container (142 g) spring mix lettuce, 3 plums, cut into wedges, 80 ml (⅓ cup) sliced almonds and 2 green onions, chopped. Toss.

1 **Ground veal**
450 g (1 lb)

2 **1 small zucchini**
grated

3 **Lemon**
15 ml (1 tbsp) zest

4 **Greek seasoning**
15 ml (1 tbsp)

5 **Tzatziki**
250 ml (1 cup)

ALSO NEEDED:
● **½ small onion**
chopped

Greek Veal and Zucchini Meatballs

Prep time **15 minutes** • Cook time **18 minutes** • Serves **4**

PER SERVING	
Calories	329
Protein	22 g
Fat	21 g
Carbohydrates	11 g
Fibre	1 g
Iron	2 mg
Calcium	89 mg
Sodium	699 mg

Preparation

1. Preheat the oven to 205°C (400°F).

2. In a bowl, mix the ground veal with the zucchini, lemon zest, Greek seasoning, a quarter of the tzatziki and the onion. Season with salt and pepper.

3. Form 16 meatballs, using about 45 ml (3 tbsp) of the mixture for each.

4. Place the meatballs on a baking sheet lined with parchment paper. Bake for 18 to 20 minutes, until the centre of the meatballs is no longer pink.

5. Serve the meatballs with the remaining tzatziki.

You can replace the ground veal with any type of ground meat!

SIDE DISH IDEA

Tomato and Feta Salad

In a salad bowl, mix 12 cocktail tomatoes, quartered, with 1 small red onion, cut into thin rounds, 1 container (200 g) of crumbled feta and 12 Kalamata olives. Add 125 ml (½ cup) herb vinaigrette and stir.

1 **Medium ground beef**
450 g (1 lb)

2 **Plain breadcrumbs**
60 ml (¼ cup)

3 **Ketchup**
45 ml (3 tbsp)

4 **Evaporated milk**
250 ml (1 cup)

5 **Yellow Cheddar**
shredded
250 g (about ½ lb)

ALSO NEEDED:
- **1 egg**
- **2 onions**
  chopped

Cheeseburger Steak

Prep time **15 minutes** • Cook time **14 minutes** • Serves **4**

PER SERVING	
Calories	692
Protein	43 g
Fat	48 g
Carbohydrates	20 g
Fibre	1 g
Iron	3 mg
Calcium	683 mg
Sodium	780 mg

Preparation

1. In a bowl, mix the ground beef with the breadcrumbs, ketchup and egg. Season with salt and pepper.

2. Shape the mixture into four patties.

3. Heat a little olive oil in a frying pan over medium heat. Cook the patties for 10 to 12 minutes, turning them occasionally, until the centre is no longer pink. Set aside on a plate.

4. In a pot, bring the evaporated milk to a boil. Remove from heat. Add the Cheddar and stir until melted. Set aside.

5. Heat a little olive oil in the pan over medium heat. Cook the onions for 4 to 5 minutes. Season with salt and pepper.

6. Top the patties with the cheese sauce and onions.

SIDE DISH IDEA

Oven Fries

Cut 5 large potatoes into sticks. In a bowl, mix the potato sticks with 30 ml (2 tbsp) olive oil, 15 ml (1 tbsp) chopped fresh thyme and 15 ml (1 tbsp) steak spice. Spread the potato sticks out on a single layer on one or two baking sheets lined with parchment paper. Bake for 20 to 25 minutes at 220°C (425°F) until golden and crispy, turning the sticks at the halfway point.

FISH & SEAFOOD

Tuna, shrimp, salmon, scallops, cod... You'll be hooked on this boatload of fish and seafood recipes we've put together for you! From soups and stir-fries to tacos, rice and even quiche, they'll satisfy your every craving for seaside fare!

1
Haddock
600 g (1⅓ lb)
fillets

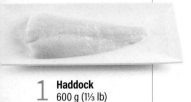

2
Taco seasoning
15 ml (1 tbsp)

3
Tortillas
8 small

4
**12 cherry
tomatoes**
various colours
cut into quarters

5
Romaine lettuce
chopped
500 ml (2 cups)

Fish Tacos

Prep time **15 minutes** • Cook time **10 minutes** • Serves **4**

PER SERVING	
Calories	339
Protein	52 g
Fat	6 g
Carbohydrates	38 g
Fibre	4 g
Iron	3 mg
Calcium	80 mg
Sodium	842 mg

Preparation

1. Preheat the oven to 205°C (400°F).

2. Place the haddock fillets on a baking sheet lined with parchment paper. Sprinkle the fillets with taco seasoning. Bake for 10 to 12 minutes.

3. Remove the haddock fillets from the oven and use a fork to break the meat into pieces.

4. Heat a frying pan over medium heat. Warm the tortillas for 15 seconds on each side.

5. Top the tortillas with fish, tomatoes, lettuce and red onion.

 You can replace the haddock with any other variety of white fish, or salmon or trout.

A LITTLE EXTRA

Avocado Lime Sauce

In a bowl, mix 1 cubed avocado, 125 ml (½ cup) sour cream, 30 ml (2 tbsp) chopped fresh cilantro and 15 ml (1 tbsp) fresh lime juice. Season with salt and pepper. Use an immersion blender to mix until smooth.

ALSO NEEDED:
● **1 small red onion**
  sliced into thin rounds

1 **Medium shrimp**
(31–40 per pound)
raw and peeled
1 bag (340 g)

2 **Frozen stir-fry
vegetable mix**
450 g (1 lb)

3 **Red curry paste**
30 ml (2 tbsp)

4 **Coconut milk**
250 ml (1 cup)

ALSO NEEDED:
● **Garlic**
minced
15 ml (1 tbsp)

OPTIONAL:
● **Ginger**
grated
15 ml (1 tbsp)

5 **Fish sauce**
15 ml (1 tbsp)

Thai Shrimp Stir-Fry

Prep time **15 minutes** • Cook time **7 minutes** • Serves **4**

Preparation

1. Heat a little canola oil in a frying pan over medium heat.
Cook the shrimp for 1 minute on each side.

2. Add the vegetables, garlic, and ginger if desired.
Cook for 1 minute, stirring.

3. Add the curry paste and cook for 30 seconds, until fragrant.

4. Add the coconut milk and fish sauce. Bring to a boil and cook
for 3 to 4 minutes.

⇨ Check out our recipe for a homemade stir-fry vegetable mix
on page 25.

PER SERVING	
Calories	218
Protein	16 g
Fat	11 g
Carbohydrates	14 g
Fibre	4 g
Iron	4 mg
Calcium	86 mg
Sodium	1,363 mg

SIDE DISH IDEA

Lime Rice Vermicelli

Soak 150 g (⅓ lb) rice vermicelli
according to the instructions on
the package. Drain. Heat 15 ml
(1 tbsp) sesame oil (untoasted)
in a pan over medium heat. Cook
125 ml (½ cup) shallots, chopped,
for 1 minute. Add the zest and juice from
1 lime, 30 ml (2 tbsp) chopped fresh cilantro, the rice
vermicelli and 80 ml (⅓ cup) vegetable stock. Season
with salt and pepper, and stir. Cook for 1 minute.

1 **Almonds**
chopped
125 ml (½ cup)

2 **Plain breadcrumbs**
80 ml (⅓ cup)

3 **Salmon**
4 fillets, 150 g
(⅓ lb) each,
skin removed

4 **Honey**
15 ml (1 tbsp)

5 **1 lemon**
cut into wedges

Almond-Crusted Salmon

Prep time **15 minutes** • Cook time **12 minutes** • Serves **4**

Preparation

1. Preheat the oven to 205°C (400°F).

2. Combine the almonds and breadcrumbs in a bowl. Season with salt and pepper.

3. Place the salmon fillets on a baking sheet lined with parchment paper. Drizzle with honey and top with the almond mixture.

4. Bake for 12 to 15 minutes. Serve with lemon wedges.

 You can replace the almonds with pecans or walnuts!

PER SERVING	
Calories	443
Protein	35 g
Fat	27 g
Carbohydrates	15 g
Fibre	2 g
Iron	1 mg
Calcium	64 mg
Sodium	158 mg

SIDE DISH IDEA

Wild Rice Pilaf with Herbs

Pour 250 ml (1 cup) wild rice into a pot. Cover the rice with cold, salted water. Bring to a boil, then cover and let simmer for 40 to 50 minutes, until tender. Heat 15 ml (1 tbsp) olive oil in another pot over medium heat. Cook 1 chopped onion, 15 ml (1 tbsp) minced garlic and 1 diced carrot for 2 to 3 minutes. Add the wild rice, 15 ml (1 tbsp) chopped fresh thyme and 10 ml (2 tsp) chopped fresh rosemary. Season with salt and pepper. Heat for 1 to 2 minutes. Add 60 ml (¼ cup) chopped fresh parsley and stir.

1 **Condensed cream
of mushroom soup**
2 cans (284 ml each)

2 **Rice**
cooked
500 ml (2 cups)

3 **Green peas**
375 ml (1½ cups)

4 **Tuna**
drained
3 cans (170 g each)

5 **Monterey Jack**
grated
375 ml (1½ cups)

Tuna Rice Casserole

Prep time **15 minutes** • Cook time **20 minutes** • Serves **4**

PER SERVING	
Calories	586
Protein	46 g
Fat	25 g
Carbohydrates	46 g
Fibre	5 g
Iron	4 mg
Calcium	407 mg
Sodium	1,584 mg

Preparation

1. Preheat the oven to 205°C (400°F).

2. Bring the cream of mushroom soup and 500 ml (2 cups) of water to a boil in a pot. Add the cooked rice, green peas and tuna. Stir.

3. Transfer the mixture to a 23 cm (9 in) baking dish. Cover with Monterey Jack. Bake for 20 to 25 minutes.

 For an even creamier casserole, you can replace the water with the same amount of milk!

SIDE DISH IDEA

Sautéed Mushrooms and Spinach

In a frying pan, melt 30 ml (2 tbsp) butter over medium heat. Cook 1 package (227 g) of sliced mushrooms and 5 sliced oyster mushrooms for 3 to 4 minutes. Add 1 sliced onion, 2 cloves of garlic, minced, and 500 ml (2 cups) baby spinach. Cook for 1 minute. Add 15 ml (1 tbsp) cider vinegar and 15 ml (1 tbsp) chopped fresh tarragon. Stir.

1 **Garlic butter**
80 ml (⅓ cup)

2 **1 lemon**
zest and juice

3 **Green and yellow beans**
cut into pieces
300 g (⅔ lb)

4 **Tilapia**
4 fillets, 150 g
(⅓ lb) each

5 **Northern shrimp**
150 g (250 ml)

Northern Shrimp and Tilapia Foil Packs

Prep time **15 minutes** • Cook time **18 minutes** • Serves **4**

PER SERVING	
Calories	340
Protein	38 g
Fat	19 g
Carbohydrates	8 g
Fibre	2 g
Iron	2 mg
Calcium	54 mg
Sodium	522 mg

Preparation

1. Preheat the oven to 205°C (400°F).

2. In a microwave-safe bowl, melt the garlic butter with the lemon zest and juice in the microwave.

3. Set out four large sheets of aluminum foil. Distribute the beans into the centre of each sheet. Place a fillet of tilapia on each portion of beans. Top with shrimp, then drizzle with the garlic butter.

4. Fold the aluminum foil to form airtight packets.

5. Place the foil packs onto one or two baking sheets. Bake for 18 to 20 minutes.

 You can replace the tilapia with another variety of white fish, either firm (mahi-mahi, halibut, etc.) or semi-firm (bass, cod, haddock, sole, turbot, etc.).

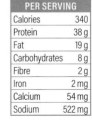

A LITTLE EXTRA
Crunchy Pancetta

Heat a frying pan over medium heat. Brown 1 package of cooked diced pancetta (175 g) for 1 to 2 minutes. Add 80 ml (⅓ cup) slivered almonds and 30 ml (2 tbsp) chopped fresh chives. Stir and cook for 30 seconds.

1 **Salmon**
4 fillets, 150 g
(⅓ lb) each,
skin removed

2 **Sliced pineapples**
drained
1 can (540 ml)

3 **Sugar snap peas**
150 g (⅓ lb)

4 **3 pepper halves**
various colours
chopped

5 **Thick teriyaki
sauce**
125 ml (½ cup)

ALSO NEEDED:
- **1 onion**
  cut into quarters
- **Sesame oil (untoasted)**
  30 ml (2 tbsp)

Sheet Pan Salmon Teriyaki

Prep time **15 minutes** • Cook time **18 minutes** • Serves **4**

PER SERVING	
Calories	534
Protein	34 g
Fat	27 g
Carbohydrates	38 g
Fibre	5 g
Iron	2 mg
Calcium	52 mg
Sodium	720 mg

Preparation

1. Preheat the oven to 205°C (400°F).

2. Cut the pineapple slices in half.

3. Place the salmon fillets on a baking sheet lined with parchment paper. Spread the pineapple slices, sugar snap peas, peppers and onion around the salmon fillets.

4. Combine the teriyaki sauce and sesame oil in a bowl.

5. Drizzle the teriyaki sauce mixture over the salmon, pineapple and vegetables. Bake for 18 to 20 minutes.

 You can replace the sesame oil with olive or canola oil!

SIDE DISH IDEA

Cilantro Rice Noodles

Soak 200 g (about ½ lb) large rice noodles according to the instructions on the packaging. Bring 80 ml (⅓ cup) vegetable stock to a boil in a pot. Add the rice noodles, 2 chopped green onions, ½ chopped Thai chili pepper, 15 ml (1 tbsp) oyster sauce and 30 ml (2 tbsp) chopped fresh cilantro. Reheat for 1 minute, stirring.

1 **25 jumbo shrimp**
(21-25 per pound)
raw and peeled

2 **Caesar dressing**
store-bought
180 ml (¾ cup)

3 **¼ baguette**
cut into small
cubes

4 **1 romaine lettuce**
shredded

5 **Bacon**
4 slices, cooked
cut into pieces

OPTIONAL:
● **Parmesan**
grated
125 ml (½ cup)

Shrimp Caesar Salad

Prep time **15 minutes** • Cook time **4 minutes** • Serves **4**

PER SERVING	
Calories	552
Protéines	29 g
Matières grasses	47 g
Glucides	12 g
Fibres	2 g
Fer	2 mg
Calcium	270 mg
Sodium	1,699 mg

Preparation

1. Heat a little olive oil in a frying pan over medium heat. Cook the shrimp for 1 minute on each side.

2. Add a quarter of the Caesar dressing and stir. Remove from heat and set aside.

3. Heat a little olive oil in another pan over medium heat. Brown the bread cubes for 2 to 3 minutes.

4. In a salad bowl, mix the lettuce with the shrimp, bacon, croutons, remaining dressing, and Parmesan if desired.

HOMEMADE VERSION
Caesar Dressing

In a bowl, place 125 ml (½ cup) mayonnaise, 60 ml (¼ cup) plain yogurt, 60 ml (¼ cup) grated Parmesan, 15 ml (1 tbsp) fresh lemon juice and 10 ml (2 tsp) minced garlic. Season with pepper. Use an immersion blender to mix until smooth.

1 **Mayonnaise**
125 ml (½ cup)

2 **Tuna**
drained
3 cans (170 g each)

3 **Vegetable crackers**
crushed into
breadcrumbs
180 ml (¾ cup)

4 **Lime**
15 ml (1 tbsp)
of zest

5 **Fresh cilantro**
chopped
30 ml (2 tbsp)

ALSO NEEDED:
• **1 egg**

Cilantro Lime Tuna Croquettes

Prep time **15 minutes** • Cook time **4 minutes** • Serves **4**

PER SERVING	
Calories	403
Protein	27 g
Fat	27 g
Carbohydrates	12 g
Fibre	2 g
Iron	2 mg
Calcium	30 mg
Sodium	348 mg

Preparation

1. In a bowl, combine the mayonnaise, tuna, cracker breadcrumbs, zest, cilantro and egg. Season with salt and pepper.

2. Shape the mixture into eight patties.

3. Heat a little canola oil in a frying pan over medium heat. Cook the croquettes for 2 to 3 minutes on each side.

 You can replace the vegetable crackers with your choice of flavoured crackers!

┌ **A LITTLE EXTRA**

Curry Yogurt Sauce

Combine 180 ml (¾ cup) plain Greek yogurt with 2 chopped green onions and 2.5 ml (½ tsp) curry powder. Season with salt and pepper.

1 **California blend frozen vegetables**
750 ml (3 cups)

2 **Alfredo sauce**
625 ml (2½ cups)

3 **Frozen seafood cocktail mix**
thawed
1 package (454 g)

4 **Salmon**
300 g (⅔ lb)
of fillets, skin
removed and cut
into small cubes

5 **Mozzarella**
shredded
500 ml (2 cups)

OPTIONAL:
● **Fresh basil**
chopped
45 ml (3 tbsp)

Seafood Gratin

Prep time **15 minutes** • Cook time **25 minutes** • Serves **4**

PER SERVING	
Calories	718
Protein	58 g
Fat	41 g
Carbohydrates	24 g
Fibre	4 g
Iron	6 mg
Calcium	491 mg
Sodium	2,225 mg

Preparation

1. Preheat the oven to 205°C (400°F).

2. Cook the vegetable blend for 5 minutes in a pot of boiling salted water. Drain.

3. In the same pot, bring the Alfredo sauce to a boil. Add the vegetables, seafood, salmon, and basil if desired. Stir.

4. Transfer the prepared ingredients to a 33 cm x 23 cm (13 in x 9 in) baking dish. Top with mozzarella. Bake for 20 to 25 minutes.

💡 You can create your own seafood mix by selecting your favourites: cooked shrimp, raw scallops, cooked mussels, cooked lobster, cooked crab, etc.

SIDE DISH IDEA

Lemon Pasta

Cook 350 g (about ¾ lb) fettucine noodles *al dente* in a pot of boiling salted water. Drain. Melt 30 ml (2 tbsp) butter in the same pot over medium heat. Cook 3 finely chopped shallots and 30 ml (2 tbsp) lemon zest for 1 to 2 minutes. Add the pasta. Season with salt and pepper, and stir. Heat for 1 minute.

1 **8 eggs**

2 **2% milk**
80 ml (⅓ cup)

3 **Cream cheese**
softened
½ container (250 g)

4 **Smoked salmon**
cut into pieces
2 packages
(120 g each)

5 **1 small red onion**
diced

OPTIONAL:
● **Fresh dill**
chopped
30 ml (2 tbsp)

Smoked Salmon
Mini Quiches

Prep time **15 minutes** • Cook time **25 minutes** • Serves **4**

Preparation

1. Preheat the oven to 190°C (375°F).

2. In a bowl, whisk together the eggs, cream, and dill if desired. Season with salt and pepper.

3. Grease all 12 cups of a muffin tin and evenly divide the smoked salmon and onion among them. Cover with the egg mixture.

4. Bake for 20 to 30 minutes, until the quiches are set.

PER SERVING	
Calories	409
Protein	34 g
Fat	28 g
Carbohydrates	5 g
Fibre	0 g
Iron	2 mg
Calcium	121 mg
Sodium	642 mg

SIDE DISH IDEA

Prosciutto, Tomato and Caper Salad

In a salad bowl, whisk together 125 ml (½ cup) ranch dressing and 45 ml (3 tbsp) plain yogurt. Add 1 head of romaine lettuce cut into pieces, 18 cherry tomatoes of various colours cut in half, 15 ml (1 tbsp) capers, 2 chopped green onions and 4 slices of prosciutto cut into pieces. Stir.

1 **Pollock**
shredded
150 g (⅓ lb)

2 **Cream cheese**
softened
½ package (250 g)

3 **Fish seasoning**
15 ml (1 tbsp)

4 **Sole**
8 fillets, 80 g
(about 2¾ oz) each

5 **Plain breadcrumbs**
80 ml (⅓ cup)

OPTIONAL:
 3 green onions
chopped

Pollock-Stuffed Sole

Prep time **15 minutes** • Cook time **15 minutes** • Serves **4**

PER SERVING	
Calories	305
Protein	26 g
Fat	14 g
Carbohydrates	18 g
Fibre	1 g
Iron	1 mg
Calcium	91 mg
Sodium	810 mg

Preparation

1. Preheat the oven to 205°C (400°F).

2. In a bowl, mix the pollock with the cream cheese, fish seasoning, and green onions if desired.

3. Spread the pollock mixture onto the base of each sole fillet. Roll the fillets up tightly and secure with a toothpick.

4. Place the sole fillets on a baking sheet lined with parchment paper, closure facing down. Sprinkle with breadcrumbs and drizzle with olive oil. Bake for 15 to 18 minutes.

You can replace the pollock with canned crab or salmon!

SIDE DISH IDEA

Broccoli Salad

In a salad bowl, combine 125 ml (½ cup) mayonnaise with 30 ml (2 tbsp) cider vinegar and 15 ml (1 tbsp) honey. Season with salt and pepper. Add 1 small red onion, diced, 1 head of broccoli cut into small florets and 80 ml (⅓ cup) sliced almonds. Stir.

1 **Medium shrimp**
(31–40 per pound)
raw and peeled
1 bag (340 g)

2 **3 pepper halves**
various colours
diced

3 **Corn kernels**
375 ml (1½ cups)

4 **Chili powder**
15 ml (1 tbsp)

5 **Lime**
60 ml (¼ cup) juice

ALSO NEEDED:
• **1 small red onion**
diced

OPTIONAL:
• **½ jalapeño**
seeded and chopped

Chili Lime Shrimp

Prep time **15 minutes** • Cook time **6 minutes** • Serves **4**

Preparation

1. Heat a little olive oil in a frying pan over medium heat. Cook the shrimp for 3 to 4 minutes.

2. Add the peppers, corn, onion, and jalapeño if desired. Sprinkle with chili powder. Stir. Cook for 3 to 4 minutes.

3. Add the lime juice and stir.

PER SERVING	
Calories	175
Protein	15 g
Fat	5 g
Carbohydrates	21 g
Fibre	3 g
Iron	1 mg
Calcium	67 mg
Sodium	512 mg

A LITTLE EXTRA

Cilantro Sour Cream

Combine 180 ml (¾ cup) sour cream, 40 ml (2 tbsp) chopped fresh cilantro, 5 ml (1 tsp) honey, 15 ml (1 tbsp) lime zest and 5 ml (1 tsp) garlic powder. Season with salt and pepper.

1 **3 pepper halves**
various colours
diced

2 **2 avocados**
diced

3 **Tuna**
drained
2 cans (170 g each)

4 **Chickpeas**
rinsed and drained
1 can (540 ml)

5 **Catalina dressing**
store-bought
125 ml (½ cup)

ALSO NEEDED:
● **1 small red onion**
diced
OPTIONAL:
● **1 head Boston lettuce**

Tuna Chickpea Salad

Prep time **15 minutes** • Serves **4**

PER SERVING	
Calories	441
Protein	34 g
Fat	24 g
Carbohydrates	47 g
Fibre	12 g
Iron	5 mg
Calcium	89 mg
Sodium	355 mg

Preparation

1. In a salad bowl, mix the peppers with the avocado, tuna, chickpeas, red onion and dressing.

2. If desired, place Boston lettuce leaves in bowls and top with chickpea salad.

 You can replace the chickpeas with red, black or white beans!

HOMEMADE VERSION

Catalina Dressing

In a bowl, place 80 ml (⅓ cup) red wine vinegar, 80 ml (⅓ cup) ketchup, 60 ml (¼ cup) honey, 15 ml (1 tbsp) paprika, 5 ml (1 tsp) Worcestershire sauce, 15 ml (1 tbsp) onion powder and 125 ml (½ cup) olive oil. Season with salt and pepper. Use an immersion blender to mix.

1 **Salmon**
4 fillets, 150 g
(⅓ lb) each,
skin removed

2 **1 lemon**
zest and juice

3 **Mayonnaise**
125 ml (½ cup)

4 **Plain Greek
yogurt (0%)**
80 ml (⅓ cup)

5 **Fresh dill**
chopped
15 ml (1 tbsp)

ALSO NEEDED:
● **Olive oil**
30 ml (2 tbsp)

OPTIONAL:
● **2 green onions**
chopped

Salmon Fillets with Lemon Dill Sauce

Prep time **15 minutes** • Cook time **15 minutes** • Serves **4**

PER SERVING	
Calories	597
Protein	33 g
Fat	50 g
Carbohydrates	2 g
Fibre	0 g
Iron	1 mg
Calcium	50 mg
Sodium	257 mg

Preparation

1. Preheat the oven to 205°C (400°F).

2. Place the salmon fillets on a baking sheet lined with parchment paper.

3. In a bowl, combine the lemon zest and oil. Season with salt and pepper.

4. Brush the salmon fillets with the lemon oil. Bake for 15 to 18 minutes.

5. In another bowl, mix the lemon juice with the mayonnaise, yogurt, dill, and green onions if desired. Serve with the salmon.

 You can replace the fresh dill with 5 ml (1 tsp) of dried dill!

SIDE DISH IDEA

Asparagus and Tomatoes with Bacon

In a bowl, mix 300 g (⅓ lb) asparagus cut into pieces with 12 cherry tomatoes, cut in half, and 8 slices of precooked bacon, cut into pieces. Spread the mixture over a baking sheet lined with parchment paper. Bake for 10 to 12 minutes at 205°C (400°F).

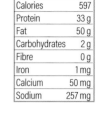

1 **24 small shrimp**
(71–90 per pound)
raw and peeled

2 **Frozen mixed
vegetables**
500 ml (2 cups)

3 **White rice**
cooked
500 ml (2 cups)

4 **2 eggs**
beaten

5 **Teriyaki
marinade sauce**
60 ml (¼ cup)

ALSO NEEDED:
• **Garlic**
minced
15 ml (1 tbsp)

OPTIONAL:
• **3 green onions**
chopped

Shrimp Fried Rice

Prep time **15 minutes** • Cook time **7 minutes** • Serves **4**

Preparation

1. Heat a little canola oil in a large frying pan or wok over medium-high heat. Cook the shrimp for 2 to 3 minutes.

2. Add the mixed vegetables and garlic. Cook for 2 minutes.

3. Add the cooked rice and cook for 2 to 3 minutes, stirring.

4. Drizzle in the beaten eggs and cook for 1 to 2 minutes, stirring, until the eggs are set.

5. Add the teriyaki sauce and stir.

6. Garnish with green onion before serving if desired.

⇨ Check out our recipe for homemade frozen mixed vegetables on page 25.

PER SERVING	
Calories	250
Protein	16 g
Fat	8 g
Carbohydrates	38 g
Fibre	4 g
Iron	2 mg
Calcium	81 mg
Sodium	871 mg

A LITTLE EXTRA

Spicy Sauce

Combine 125 ml (½ cup) mayonnaise with 15 ml (1 tbsp) fresh lime juice, 5 ml (1 tsp) sriracha, 15 ml (1 tbsp) honey and 30 ml (2 tbsp) water.

1 **Shallots**
chopped
125 ml (½ cup)

2 **Bacon**
10 slices, cooked
and chopped

3 **Cooking
cream (15%)**
250 ml (1 cup)

4 **Parmesan**
grated
125 ml (½ cup)

5 **24 medium
scallops**
(20–30 per pound)

ALSO NEEDED:
● **Butter**
30 ml (2 tbsp)

OPTIONAL:
● **Fresh chives**
30 ml (2 tbsp), chopped

Scallops with Creamy Bacon Sauce

Prep time **15 minutes** · Cook time **3 minutes** · Serves **4**

PER SERVING	
Calories	340
Protein	23 g
Fat	23 g
Carbohydrates	11 g
Fibre	0 g
Iron	1 mg
Calcium	238 mg
Sodium	844 mg

Preparation

1. Melt half of the butter in a pot over medium heat. Cook the shallots and bacon for 1 minute.

2. Add the cream. Season with salt and pepper, and stir. Bring to a boil.

3. Add the Parmesan and stir until melted.

4. If desired, add the chives and stir. Keep warm.

5. Season the scallops with salt and pepper.

6. Melt the rest of the butter in a frying pan over medium heat. Brown the scallops for 1 minute on each side. Serve with the sauce.

 You can replace the scallops with cooked shrimp (31–40 per pound)!

SIDE DISH IDEA

Asparagus and Pecan Sauté

Heat 15 ml (1 tbsp) olive oil in a frying pan over medium heat. Cook 450 g (1 lb) asparagus, cut into pieces, for 4 to 5 minutes. Add 125 ml (½ cup) coarsely chopped pecans and 80 ml (⅓ cup) maple syrup. Season with salt and pepper. Cook for 1 minute.

1 **Salmon**
4 fillets, 150 g
(⅓ lb) each,
skin removed

2 **Sour cream (14%)**
125 ml (½ cup)

3 **Dijon mustard**
15 ml (1 tbsp)

4 **3 green onions**
chopped

5 **Italian shredded
cheese blend**
375 ml (1½ cups)

Cheesy Baked Salmon

Prep time **15 minutes** • Cook time **18 minutes** • Serves **4**

PER SERVING	
Calories	495
Protein	43 g
Fat	34 g
Carbohydrates	3 g
Fibre	0 g
Iron	1 mg
Calcium	316 mg
Sodium	385 mg

Preparation

1. Preheat the oven to 205°C (400°F).

2. Place the salmon fillets on a baking sheet lined with parchment paper.

3. Mix the sour cream, mustard and green onions in a bowl. Season with salt and pepper.

4. Spread the sour cream mixture over the salmon fillets. Top with cheese. Bake for 18 to 20 minutes.

SIDE DISH IDEA

Mushroom Rice

In a pot, melt 15 ml (1 tbsp) butter over medium heat. Cook 1 package of sliced mushrooms (227 g) and 1 chopped onion for 2 minutes. Add 250 ml (1 cup) basmati rice, rinsed and drained. Stir. Pour in 500 ml (2 cups) vegetable stock. Bring to a boil and let simmer over low heat for 18 to 20 minutes, until the liquid is fully absorbed.

1 **Cod**
675 g (1½ lb)
of fillets

2 **Mayonnaise**
180 ml (¾ cup)

3 **Sun-dried tomato pesto**
30 ml (2 tbsp)

4 **Cream cheese**
softened
80 ml (⅓ cup)

5 **Prosciutto**
12 slices

Prosciutto-Wrapped Cod with Sun-Dried Tomato

Prep time **15 minutes** • Cook time **10 minutes** • Serves **4**

PER SERVING	
Calories	654
Protein	45 g
Fat	50 g
Carbohydrates	3 g
Fibre	0 g
Iron	2 mg
Calcium	48 mg
Sodium	1,440 mg

Preparation

1. Preheat the oven to 205°C (400°F).

2. Slice the cod into 12 large strips.

3. Combine the mayonnaise, pesto and cream cheese in a bowl.

4. Brush the cod strips with half the pesto mayonnaise.

5. Wrap 1 slice of prosciutto around each cod strip.

6. Place the cod strips on a baking sheet lined with parchment paper, closure facing down. Bake for 10 to 12 minutes.

7. Serve the cod with the remaining pesto mayonnaise.

 You can replace the cod with another type of white fish, either medium-firm (bass, haddock, sole, turbot, etc.) or firm (tilapia, mahi-mahi, halibut, etc.).

SIDE DISH IDEA

Honey-Roasted Carrots and Green Beans

Cut 8 Nantes carrots in half lengthwise. Spread the carrots and 300 g (⅔ lb) green beans on a baking sheet lined with parchment paper. In a bowl, mix 45 ml (3 tbsp) honey with 30 ml (2 tbsp) olive oil and 15 ml (1 tbsp) chopped fresh thyme. Brush the carrots and green beans with the honey mixture. Season with salt and pepper. Bake for 18 to 20 minutes at 205°C (400°F).

1 **Flour**
125 ml (½ cup)

2 **2 eggs**

3 **Unsweetened shredded coconut**
180 ml (¾ cup)

4 **Panko breadcrumbs**
125 ml (½ cup)

5 **20 medium shrimp**
(31–40 per pound)
raw and peeled

OPTIONAL:
● **2 green onions**
chopped

Crispy Coconut Shrimp

Prep time **15 minutes** • Cook time **12 minutes** • Serves **4**

PER SERVING	
Calories	252
Protein	16 g
Fat	12 g
Carbohydrates	21 g
Fibre	2 g
Iron	2 mg
Calcium	51 mg
Sodium	384 mg

Preparation

1. Preheat the oven to 180°C (350°F).

2. Set out three shallow bowls. Put the flour in the first bowl. Beat the eggs in the second. In the third, mix the coconut, panko breadcrumbs, and green onions, if desired.

3. Coat the shrimp in flour and shake to remove excess. Dip them into the beaten eggs and then coat them in the breadcrumb mixture.

4. Place the shrimp on a baking sheet lined with parchment paper. Drizzle with olive oil. Bake for 12 to 15 minutes. Season with salt and pepper.

A LITTLE EXTRA

Pineapple Sauce

In a pot, combine 125 ml (½ cup) coconut milk with 1 can (540 ml) of crushed pineapple and 15 ml (1 tbsp) cornstarch. Season with salt and pepper. Bring to a boil, stirring, and let simmer over low heat for 2 minutes.

Maple Mustard Trout

Prep time **15 minutes** · Cook time **10 minutes** · Serves **4**

PER SERVING	
Calories	288
Protein	32 g
Fat	11 g
Carbohydrates	14 g
Fibre	0 g
Iron	2 mg
Calcium	89 mg
Sodium	475 mg

Preparation

1. Preheat the oven to 205°C (400°F).

2. In a bowl, mix the maple syrup with both types of mustard and the soy sauce. Season with salt and pepper.

3. Place the trout fillets on a baking sheet lined with parchment paper. Brush the trout fillets with the mustard mixture.

4. Bake for 9 to 11 minutes.

5. Broil for a minute.

6. Remove the baking sheet from the oven and sprinkle with chives if desired.

You can replace the brook trout with salmon!

1 **Maple syrup**
60 ml (¼ cup)

2 **Dijon mustard**
15 ml (1 tbsp)

3 **Whole-grain mustard**
15 ml (1 tbsp)

4 **Soy sauce**
15 ml (1 tbsp)

5 **Brook trout**
8 fillets, 150 g (⅓ lb) each, skin removed

OPTIONAL:
● **Fresh chives**
30 ml (2 tbsp), chopped

SIDE DISH IDEA

Lemon Broccoli and Cauliflower

In a bowl, mix 1 head of broccoli and 1 head of cauliflower, cut into florets, with 1 chopped onion, 2 minced garlic cloves, 30 ml (2 tbsp) lemon zest and 30 ml (2 tbsp) fresh lemon juice. Spread the mixture over a baking sheet lined with parchment paper. Drizzle with 30 ml (2 tbsp) olive oil. Season with salt and pepper. Bake for 20 to 25 minutes at 205°C (400°F).

1 **Haddock**
675 g (1½ lb)
of fillets

2 **Flour**
125 ml (½ cup)

3 **2 eggs**

4 **Cornmeal**
180 ml (¾ cup)

5 **Lemon and
pepper seasoning**
15 ml (1 tbsp)

Fish Sticks

Prep time **15 minutes** • Cook time **3 minutes** • Serves **4**

PER SERVING	
Calories	370
Protein	35 g
Fat	8 g
Carbohydrates	37 g
Fibre	2 g
Iron	2 mg
Calcium	42 mg
Sodium	395 mg

Preparation

1. Preheat the oven to 190°C (375°F).

2. Cut the haddock fillets into 12 strips.

3. Set out three shallow bowls. Put the flour in the first bowl. Beat the eggs in the second. In the third, mix the cornmeal with the lemon and pepper seasoning.

4. Coat the haddock in the flour and shake to remove the excess. Dip the strips into the beaten eggs, and then coat them with cornmeal.

5. Place the haddock strips on a baking sheet lined with parchment paper, leaving space between each one. Drizzle with olive oil. Bake for 20 to 25 minutes, turning the strips over at the halfway point.

You can replace the cornmeal with plain panko breadcrumbs!

A LITTLE EXTRA

Tartare Sauce

Mix 180 ml (¾ cup) mayonnaise with 30 ml (2 tbsp) chopped baby dill pickles, 15 ml (1 tbsp) chopped capers, 45 ml (3 tbsp) chopped fresh parsley and 15 ml (1 tbsp) lemon zest.

VEGETARIAN

Thanks to their versatility and their many
nutritional benefits, legumes take centre stage
in this vegetarian section, sharing the spotlight
with other important sources of protein like
tofu, eggs and a variety of delicious cheeses!

1 **Frozen diced vegetable mix**
500 ml (2 cups)

2 **Diced tomatoes with Italian spices**
1 can (796 ml)

3 **Vegetable stock**
375 ml (1½ cups)

4 **Lentils**
rinsed and drained
1 can (540 ml)

5 **Small pasta shells**
125 ml (½ cup)

OPTIONAL:
● **Fresh oregano**
chopped
30 ml (2 tbsp)

Lentil Minestrone Soup

Prep time **15 minutes** • Cook time **16 minutes** • Serves **4**

PER SERVING	
Calories	271
Protein	16 g
Fat	4 g
Carbohydrates	46 g
Fibre	9 g
Iron	7 mg
Calcium	149 mg
Sodium	288 mg

Preparation

1. Heat a little olive oil in a pot over medium heat. Cook the vegetable mix for 1 to 2 minutes.

2. Add the diced tomatoes and stock. Stir. Bring to a boil and cook for 10 minutes over low heat.

3. Add the lentils and pasta. Stir. Bring to a boil again and let simmer for 5 minutes.

4. Sprinkle with oregano before serving if desired.

⇨ Check out our recipe for homemade frozen diced vegetable mix on page 25.

A LITTLE EXTRA

Parmesan Chips

On a baking sheet lined with parchment paper, form 12 Parmesan circles, 5 cm (2 in) in diameter, with 250 ml (1 cup) grated Parmesan. Sprinkle with 15 ml (1 tbsp) Cajun spices. Bake in the oven for 8 to 10 minutes at 180°C (350°F), until the edges of the circles begin to brown.

1 **Firm tofu**
cubed
1 block (454 g)

2 **Ginger**
minced
15 ml (1 tbsp)

3 **1 onion**
chopped

4 **Frozen stir-fry
vegetables mix**
thawed and drained
500 ml (2 cups)

5 **Thick teriyaki
sauce**
125 ml (½ cup)

ALSO NEEDED:
● **Garlic**
minced
15 ml (1 tbsp)

OPTIONAL:
● **Sesame seeds**
15 ml (1 tbsp)

Teriyaki Tofu Stir-Fry

Prep time **15 minutes** • Cook time **6 minutes** • Serves **4**

Preparation

1. Heat a little olive oil in a large frying pan over medium heat. Brown the tofu cubes for 2 to 3 minutes on each side.

2. Add the ginger, onion and garlic. Stir. Cook for 1 minute.

3. Add the vegetables and stir. Cook for 2 to 3 minutes.

4. Pour in the teriyaki sauce. Bring to a boil and cook for 1 minute.

5. Sprinkle with sesame seeds before serving if desired.

⇨ Check out our recipe for a homemade stir-fry vegetable mix on page 25.

PER SERVING	
Calories	353
Protein	23 g
Fat	18 g
Carbohydrates	27 g
Fibre	5 g
Iron	4 mg
Calcium	150 mg
Sodium	668 mg

SIDE DISH IDEA

Fried Rice Vermicelli

Soak 150 g (⅓ lb) rice vermicelli according to the instructions on the package. Drain. Heat 15 ml (1 tbsp) canola oil in a frying pan over medium heat. Cook 2 cloves of minced garlic for 30 seconds. Add 15 ml (1 tbsp) soy sauce, 3 chopped green onions, the rice vermicelli and 1 chopped Thai chili pepper. Stir. Cook for 1 to 2 minutes.

1 **8 eggs**

2 **Oka cheese**
grated
375 ml (1½ cups)

3 **Baguette**
cubed
1 litre (4 cups)

4 **Baby spinach**
500 ml (2 cups)

5 **Mushrooms**
sliced
1 package (227 g)

ALSO NEEDED:
● **2% milk**
125 ml (½ cup)

Egg and Veggie Casserole

Prep time **15 minutes** • Cook time **30 minutes** • Serves **4**

PER SERVING	
Calories	546
Protein	32 g
Fat	28 g
Carbohydrates	43 g
Fibre	4 g
Iron	3 mg
Calcium	454 mg
Sodium	812 mg

Preparation

1. Preheat the oven to 205°C (400°F).

2. In a bowl, whisk together the eggs, cheese and milk.

3. Add the bread cubes, spinach and mushrooms to the bowl. Season with salt and pepper, and stir.

4. Grease a 33 cm x 23 cm (13 in x 9 in) baking dish and pour the egg mixture into it.

5. Bake for 30 to 35 minutes, until the casserole is set.

You can replace the baguette with any type of crusty bread!

SIDE DISH IDEA

Tomato Salad

Quarter 16 cocktail tomatoes of various colours. Thinly slice 1 small red onion. Place the tomatoes and onion in a salad bowl and add 125 ml (½ cup) sliced black olives, 60 ml (¼ cup) olive oil and 15 ml (1 tbsp) balsamic vinegar. Season with salt and pepper, and stir.

1 **4 sweet potatoes**
peeled and cubed

2 **3 pepper halves**
various colours
cubed

3 **Haloumi**
(grilling cheese)
cubed
250 g (about ½ lb)

4 **Chickpeas**
rinsed and drained
1 can (540 ml)

5 **Italian vinaigrette**
125 ml (½ cup)

ALSO NEEDED:
- **1 small red onion**
  cut into wedges

Roasted Chickpeas, Haloumi and Vegetables

Prep time **15 minutes** • Cook time **25 minutes** • Serves **4**

PER SERVING	
Calories	553
Protein	24 g
Fat	25 g
Carbohydrates	61 g
Fibre	9 g
Iron	4 mg
Calcium	682 mg
Sodium	1,078 mg

Preparation

1. Preheat the oven to 205°C (400°F).

2. Spread the sweet potatoes, peppers, haloumi, chickpeas and onion over a baking sheet lined with parchment paper. Drizzle with vinaigrette.

3. Bake for 25 to 30 minutes, stirring the ingredients at the halfway point.

 You can replace the Italian vinaigrette with balsamic, Greek or sun-dried tomato vinaigrette!

SIDE DISH IDEA

Sun-Dried Tomato Rice

Heat 15 ml (1 tbsp) olive oil in a pot over medium heat. Cook 1 diced onion and 15 ml (1 tbsp) minced garlic for 2 minutes. Add 250 ml (1 cup) long grain white rice, 80 ml (⅓ cup) sun-dried tomatoes, chopped, and 500 ml (2 cups) vegetable stock. Season with salt and pepper, and stir. Bring to a boil, then cover and cook over medium-low heat for 20 to 25 minutes, until the liquid is completely absorbed.

1 **1 onion**
chopped

2 **Vegetable stock**
750 ml (3 cups)

3 **Sharp yellow Cheddar**
shredded
500 ml (2 cups)

4 **Light cream cheese**
1 package (250 g)

5 **1 head of broccoli**
cut into small florets

Broccoli Cheddar Soup

Prep time **15 minutes** • Cook time **4 minutes** • Serves **4**

PER SERVING	
Calories	501
Protein	23 g
Fat	36 g
Carbohydrates	22 g
Fibre	2 g
Iron	1 mg
Calcium	521 mg
Sodium	1,201 mg

Preparation

1. Melt the butter in a pot over medium heat. Cook the onion for 1 minute.

2. Sprinkle with flour and stir. Pour in the stock and bring to a boil, stirring.

3. Add the cheddar and cream cheese, and stir until they are melted.

4. Add the broccoli and stir. Cook for 3 to 4 minutes. Season with salt and pepper.

A LITTLE EXTRA

Garlic Croutons

Cube 1 baguette. In a bowl, mix 80 ml (⅓ cup) melted butter with 15 ml (1 tbsp) minced garlic and 45 ml (3 tbsp) chopped fresh parsley. Add the bread cubes. Season with salt and pepper, and stir. Spread the bread cubes over a baking sheet lined with parchment paper. Bake for 8 to 10 minutes at 205°C (400°F), stirring occasionally.

ALSO NEEDED:
● **Butter**
30 ml (2 tbsp)
● **Flour**
60 ml (¼ cup)

1 **Panko breadcrumbs**
250 ml (1 cup)

2 **Barbecue seasoning**
15 ml (1 tbsp)

3 **Mayonnaise**
125 ml (½ cup)

4 **Honey**
15 ml (1 tbsp)

5 **Firm tofu**
cut into large cubes
1 block (454 g)

Crispy Barbecue Tofu

Prep time **15 minutes** • Cook time **25 minutes** • Serves **4**

PER SERVING	
Calories	450
Protein	21 g
Fat	32 g
Carbohydrates	19 g
Fibre	2 g
Iron	3 mg
Calcium	100 mg
Sodium	207 mg

Preparation

1. Preheat the oven to 205°C (400°F).

2. In a bowl, mix the breadcrumbs with the barbecue seasoning.

3. In another bowl, mix the mayonnaise with the honey.

4. Dip the tofu cubes into the mayonnaise mixture, and then coat them with the breadcrumb mixture.

5. Place the tofu cubes on a baking sheet lined with parchment paper. Bake for 25 to 30 minutes.

SIDE DISH IDEA

Quinoa Salad

In a pot, place 250 ml (1 cup) quinoa, rinsed and drained, and 375 ml (1½ cups) water. Season with salt and pepper. Bring to a boil, then cover and let simmer for 18 to 20 minutes, until the liquid is completely absorbed. Transfer the quinoa to a bowl and let cool. In a salad bowl, place 180 ml (¾ cup) Italian vinaigrette, 12 cherry tomatoes, cut in half, ¼ of an English cucumber, diced, 2 chopped green onions and 2 oranges, peeled and supremed. Add the quinoa and stir.

1 **Greek vinaigrette**
store-bought
125 ml (½ cup)

2 **Mixed beans**
rinsed and drained
1 can (540 ml)

3 **English cucumber**
diced

4 **18 cherry
tomatoes**
cut in half

5 **Feta**
diced
1 container (200 g)

Greek Bean Salad

Prep time **15 minutes** • Serves **4**

PER SERVING	
Calories	418
Protein	17 g
Fat	23 g
Carbohydrates	37 g
Fibre	9 g
Iron	3 mg
Calcium	329 mg
Sodium	1,484 mg

Preparation

1. In a salad bowl, place the vinaigrette, beans, cucumber, tomatoes, feta, onion, and Kalamata olives if desired. Season with salt and pepper, and stir.

 You can replace the mixed beans with any other type of legume!

HOMEMADE VERSION
Greek Vinaigrette

In a bowl, mix 60 ml (¼ cup) olive oil with 30 ml (2 tbsp) fresh lemon juice, 30 ml (2 tbsp) chopped fresh oregano, 30 ml (2 tbsp) chopped fresh mint and 15 ml (1 tbsp) lemon zest. Season with salt and pepper, and stir.

ALSO NEEDED:
● **1 small red onion**
  cut into thin rounds
OPTIONAL:
● **16 Kalamata olives**

1 **Quinoa**
rinsed and drained
375 ml (1½ cups)

2 **Rosée sauce**
500 ml (2 cups)

3 **Shallots**
chopped
125 ml (½ cup)

4 **3 large tomatoes**
sliced

5 **Fresh mozzarella**
sliced
300 g (⅔ lb)

OPTIONAL:
● **Fresh basil**
16 small leaves

Quinoa Caprese Casserole

Prep time **15 minutes** • Cook time **43 minutes** • Serves **4**

PER SERVING	
Calories	592
Protein	23 g
Fat	28 g
Carbohydrates	65 g
Fibre	9 g
Iron	4 mg
Calcium	414 mg
Sodium	690 mg

Preparation

1. Preheat the oven to 205°C (400°F).

2. In a pot, place the quinoa and 500 ml (2 cups) of water. Season with salt and pepper. Bring to a boil, then cover and let simmer for 18 to 20 minutes, until the liquid is completely absorbed. Remove from heat and let cool.

3. In a bowl, mix the quinoa with the rosée sauce and shallots.

4. Grease a 33 cm x 23 cm (13 in x 9 in) baking dish and pour the quinoa mixture into it. Cover with slightly overlapping slices of tomato and mozzarella. Bake for 22 to 27 minutes.

5. Broil for 3 minutes.

6. Garnish with basil leaves before serving if desired.

 You can replace the quinoa with rice or any type of short pasta!

A LITTLE EXTRA
Balsamic Glaze

In a pot, mix 125 ml (½ cup) balsamic vinegar with 125 ml (½ cup) maple syrup and 15 ml (1 tbsp) olive oil. Bring to a boil, and then let simmer over low heat for 10 to 12 minutes, until thick like syrup.

1 **Firm tofu**
1 block (454 g)

2 **Soy sauce**
60 ml (¼ cup)

3 **Creamy peanut butter**
60 ml (¼ cup)

4 **Lime**
45 ml (3 tbsp) of juice

5 **Honey**
45 ml (3 tbsp)

ALSO NEEDED:
● **Cornstarch**
30 ml (2 tbsp)

OPTIONAL:
● **Peanuts**
chopped
60 ml (¼ cup)

Tofu with Peanut Sauce

Prep time **15 minutes** • Cook time **7 minutes** • Serves **4**

PER SERVING	
Calories	391
Protein	26 g
Fat	22 g
Carbohydrates	27 g
Fibre	3 g
Iron	4 mg
Calcium	113 mg
Sodium	967 mg

Preparation

1. Dry the tofu with paper towels and cut into small cubes.

2. Pour 30 ml (2 tbsp) of soy sauce into a bowl.

3. In another bowl, place the cornstarch.

4. Dip the tofu cubes into the soy sauce. Drain off the excess, and then coat the cubes with cornstarch. Shake to remove any excess cornstarch.

5. Heat a little olive oil in a large frying pan over medium heat. Brown the tofu cubes for 5 to 6 minutes on each side.

6. In a pot, mix the peanut butter with the lime juice, honey, the remaining soy sauce and 125 ml (½ cup) of water. Bring to a boil, and then let simmer over low heat for 2 to 3 minutes.

7. Serve the tofu with the sauce. Garnish with chopped peanuts if desired.

SIDE DISH IDEA

Vermicelli Salad

Soak 100 g (3½ oz) rice vermicelli according to the instructions on the package. Drain. Use a mandoline to cut 2 carrots into thin julienne strips. In a bowl, mix 45 ml (3 tbsp) sesame oil (untoasted) with 30 ml (2 tbsp) chopped fresh cilantro, 15 ml (1 tbsp) soy sauce, 10 ml (2 tsp) minced garlic, 30 ml (2 tbsp) honey, 15 ml (1 tbsp) lime zest and ½ chopped Thai chili pepper. Season with salt. Add the vermicelli and carrots. Stir. Refrigerate for 30 minutes before serving.

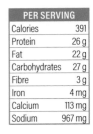

1 **2 small zucchinis**
sliced into rounds

2 **3 pepper halves**
various colours
diced

3 **Marinara sauce**
500 ml (2 cups)

4 **8 eggs**

5 **Italian shredded
cheese blend**
375 ml (1½ cups)

Italian Baked Eggs

Prep time **15 minutes** • Cook time **20 minutes** • Serves **4**

Preparation

1. Preheat the oven to 205°C (400°F).

2. Place the zucchini, pepper and onion on a generously oiled baking sheet. Bake for 10 to 12 minutes.

3. Add the marinara sauce, and oregano if desired. Season with salt and pepper. Stir to fully coat the ingredients in the sauce, and then spread them out in a single layer.

4. Use a spoon to make 8 holes in the prepared vegetables. Gently break an egg into each hole. Sprinkle with cheese.

5. Bake for another 10 to 12 minutes, until the egg whites are set.

PER SERVING	
Calories	420
Protein	26 g
Fat	27 g
Carbohydrates	20 g
Fibre	6 g
Iron	3 mg
Calcium	377 mg
Sodium	678 mg

SIDE DISH IDEA

Artichoke Heart Salad

In a salad bowl, mix 125 ml (½ cup) Tuscan Italian vinaigrette with 3 chopped green onions, 1 can (398 ml) artichoke hearts, drained and cut into wedges, 30 ml (2 tbsp) chopped fresh basil and 15 ml (1 tbsp) lemon zest. Season with salt and pepper.

ALSO NEEDED:
● **1 small red onion**
cut into wedges

OPTIONAL:
● **Oregano**
chopped
15 ml (1 tbsp)

1 **Chili seasoning**
1 packet (24 g)

2 **Quinoa**
rinsed and drained
250 ml (1 cup)

3 **Diced tomatoes**
1 can (540 ml)

4 **Corn kernels**
250 ml (1 cup)

5 **Black beans**
rinsed and drained
1 can (398 ml)

ALSO NEEDED:
● **1 onion**
  chopped

OPTIONAL:
● **Green onion**
  chopped

Quinoa Chili

Prep time **15 minutes** • Cook time **19 minutes** • Serves **4**

PER SERVING	
Calories	451
Protein	18 g
Fat	11 g
Carbohydrates	74 g
Fibre	12 g
Iron	6 mg
Calcium	111 mg
Sodium	694 mg

Preparation

1. Heat a little olive oil in a pot over medium heat. Cook the onion for 1 minute.

2. Add the chili seasoning and quinoa. Stir. Add the diced tomatoes, corn and 250 ml (1 cup) of water. Season with salt and pepper, and stir. Bring to a boil, then cover and let simmer for 9 to 10 minutes.

3. Add the black beans and cook for another 9 to 10 minutes.

4. Garnish with green onion before serving if desired.

⇨ Check out our recipe for homemade chili seasoning on page 134!

A LITTLE EXTRA
Crispy Tortilla Strips

Cut 4 tortillas into strips. Heat 125 ml (½ cup) canola oil in a frying pan over medium heat. Brown the tortilla strips a few at a time. Dry the strips on paper towels. Season with 5 ml (1 tsp) chili powder.

1 **Gnocchis**
1 package (350 g)

2 **Tomato sauce**
625 ml (2½ cups)

3 **White beans**
rinsed and drained
1 can (540 ml)

4 **Baby spinach**
1 container (142 g)

5 **Monterey Jack**
shredded
375 ml (1½ cups)

ALSO NEEDED:
● **1 onion**
chopped

Gnocchi Gratin

Prep time **15 minutes** • Cook time **12 minutes** • Serves **4**

Preparation

1. Preheat the oven to 205°C (400°F).

2. Cook the gnocchi for 1 to 2 minutes in a pot of boiling salted water. Drain.

3. Heat a little olive oil in a frying pan over medium heat. Brown the gnocchi and onion for 1 to 2 minutes. Drain.

4. Add the tomato sauce, white beans and spinach. Season with salt and pepper, and stir. Bring to a boil.

5. Pour the ingredients into a 23 cm (9 in) baking dish. Cover with Monterey Jack. Bake for 10 to 12 minutes.

You can replace the Monterey Jack with mozzarella, Cheddar or Gouda!

PER SERVING	
Calories	517
Protein	27 g
Fat	18 g
Carbohydrates	66 g
Fibre	10 g
Iron	8 mg
Calcium	509 mg
Sodium	1,380 mg

SIDE DISH IDEA

Italian Salad

In a salad bowl, mix
1 package (142 g)
of spring mix lettuce
with 8 cocktail tomatoes,
cut into quarters, 16 green olives,
1 chopped red onion and 125 ml (½ cup)
Italian vinaigrette.

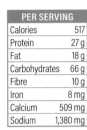

1 **Thin rice noodles**
150 g (⅓ lb)

2 **Frozen edamame**
peeled
1 bag (500 g)

3 **2 carrots**

4 **¼ head of red cabbage**

5 **Sesame vinaigrette**
store-bought
125 ml (½ cup)

OPTIONAL:
● **3 green onions**
chopped

Asian Edamame Salad

Prep time **15 minutes** · Cook time **3 minutes** · Refrigeration **30 minutes**
Serves **4**

PER SERVING	
Calories	380
Protein	16 g
Fat	12 g
Carbohydrates	55 g
Fibre	8 g
Iron	3 mg
Calcium	103 mg
Sodium	273 mg

Preparation

1. Soak the rice noodles according to the instructions on the package. Drain.

2. Cook the edamame for 3 minutes in a pot of boiling salted water. Rinse under cold water and drain.

3. Use a mandoline to cut the carrots into thin julienne strips. Finely chop the red cabbage.

4. In a salad bowl, mix the vinaigrette with the carrots, cabbage, rice noodles, edamame, and green onions if desired. Refrigerate for 30 minutes before serving.

HOMEMADE VERSION

Sesame Vinaigrette

In a bowl, place 80 ml (⅓ cup) sesame oil (untoasted), 30 ml (2 tbsp) fresh lime juice, 30 ml (2 tbsp) fresh cilantro leaves, 45 ml (3 tbsp) soy sauce, 5 ml (1 tsp) garlic powder, 10 ml (2 tsp) minced ginger and ½ chopped Thai chili pepper. Use an immersion blender to blend the ingredients until smooth.

PASTA

Looking for fresh new ways to serve pasta? We've got them right here! Leek and bacon linguine, lentil spaghetti, broccoli mac and cheese, salmon lasagna—whether you're vegetarian or a meat-lover, you won't be short on ideas thanks to this treasure trove of recipes!

1 **Macaroni**
750 ml (3 cups)

2 **Lean ground beef**
450 g (1 lb)

3 **Cream of tomato soup (ready to serve)**
1 can (540 ml)

4 **Processed cheese spread**
(like Cheez Whiz brand)
125 ml (½ cup)

5 **Soy sauce**
30 ml (2 tbsp)

ALSO NEEDED:
● **1 onion**
chopped

Cheesy Beef Macaroni

Prep time **15 minutes** · Cook time **18 minutes** · Serves **4**

PER SERVING	
Calories	767
Protein	40 g
Fat	29 g
Carbohydrates	83 g
Fibre	4 g
Iron	4 mg
Calcium	166 mg
Sodium	1,278 mg

Preparation

1. Cook the macaroni *al dente* in a pot of boiling salted water. Drain.

2. Heat a little olive oil in the same pot over medium heat. Cook the ground beef and onion for 5 to 7 minutes, breaking up the meat with a wooden spoon, until it is no longer pink.

3. Add the cream of tomato soup, processed cheese spread and soy sauce. Bring to a boil and then cook for 2 to 3 minutes, stirring occasionally.

4. Add the macaroni and stir. Season with salt and pepper. Reheat for 1 minute, stirring.

A LITTLE EXTRA

Pan-Fried Parmesan Toast

In a bowl, mix 80 ml (⅓ cup) melted butter with 30 ml (2 tbsp) grated Parmesan, 15 ml (1 tbsp) chopped fresh parsley, 10 ml (2 tsp) Cajun seasoning and 5 ml (1 tsp) minced garlic. Spread the flavoured butter on both sides of 4 slices of bread. Heat a frying pan over medium heat. Fry the slices of bread for 1 to 2 minutes on each side, until they are golden-brown.

1 **Fettuccine**
350 g (about ¾ lb)

2 **Butter**
45 ml (3 tbsp)

3 **Chicken**
3 skinless breasts,
cut into strips

4 **Cooking cream**
(15%)
500 ml (2 cups)

ALSO NEEDED:
● **Garlic**
minced
15 ml (1 tbsp)

OPTIONAL:
● **Fresh parsley**
chopped
30 ml (2 tbsp)

5 **Parmesan**
grated
180 ml (¾ cup)

Chicken Fettuccine Alfredo

Prep time **15 minutes** · Cook time **16 minutes** · Serves **4**

PER SERVING	
Calories	810
Protein	41 g
Fat	39 g
Carbohydrates	72 g
Fibre	4 g
Iron	4 mg
Calcium	362 mg
Sodium	461 mg

Preparation

1. Cook the pasta *al dente* in a pot of boiling salted water. Drain.

2. Melt the butter in the same pot over medium heat. Cook the chicken strips for 2 to 3 minutes on each side, until they are no longer pink in the centre.

3. Add the garlic and cook for 30 seconds.

4. Pour in the cream and stir. Bring to a boil.

5. Add the Parmesan and stir until melted. Add the pasta, and the parsley if desired. Season with salt and pepper. Reheat for 1 minute, stirring.

SIDE DISH IDEA

Balsamic Roasted Carrots and Brussels Sprouts

Peel 4 carrots and slice them into rounds. Cut 300 g (⅔ lb) Brussels sprouts in half. Spread the vegetables out on a baking sheet lined with parchment paper. Drizzle with 30 ml (2 tbsp) olive oil and 30 ml (2 tbsp) balsamic vinegar. Sprinkle with 15 ml (1 tbsp) chicken seasoning and stir. Bake for 25 to 30 minutes at 205°C (400°F), stirring the vegetables at the halfway point.

1 **Meat ravioli**
1 package (350 g)

2 **2 small zucchinis**
sliced into rounds

3 **Tomato sauce
with herbs**
625 ml (2½ cups)

**Italian shredded
cheese blend**
375 ml (1½ cups)

4

5 **Plain
breadcrumbs**
125 ml (½ cup)

Ravioli Casserole

Prep time **15 minutes** • Cook time **23 minutes** • Serves **4**

PER SERVING	
Calories	494
Protein	26 g
Fat	16 g
Carbohydrates	62 g
Fibre	5 g
Iron	4 mg
Calcium	354 mg
Sodium	1,176 mg

Preparation

1. Preheat the oven to 205°C (400°F).

2. Cook the ravioli and zucchini in a pot of boiling salted water for 3 minutes. Drain.

3. Put the ravioli and zucchini back in the pot. Add the tomato sauce. Season with salt and pepper, and stir.

4. Grease a 23 cm (9 in.) baking dish and add the prepared ingredients. Cover with cheese and sprinkle with breadcrumbs.

5. Bake for 20 to 25 minutes.

You can replace the meat ravioli with your favorite type of ravioli!

SIDE DISH IDEA

Light Salad

In a salad bowl, mix 80 ml (⅓ cup) plain Greek yogurt with 10 ml (2 tsp) minced garlic, 30 ml (2 tbsp) fresh lemon juice, 15 ml (1 tbsp) Worcestershire sauce and 60 ml (¼ cup) grated Parmesan. Season with salt and pepper. Add 1 head of romaine lettuce, shredded, and toss.

1 **Large pasta shells**
750 ml (3 cups)

2 **Frozen green peas**
500 ml (2 cups)

3 **Cooking cream (15%)**
375 ml (1½ cups)

4 **Dijon mustard**
30 ml (2 tbsp)

5 **Ham**
diced
450 g (1 lb)

ALSO NEEDED:
• **1 onion**
chopped

Creamy Shells with Ham and Peas

Prep time **15 minutes** • Cook time **14 minutes** • Serves **4**

PER SERVING	
Calories	596
Protein	28 g
Fat	23 g
Carbohydrates	69 g
Fibre	6 g
Iron	4 mg
Calcium	126 mg
Sodium	1,535 mg

Preparation

1. Cook the pasta *al dente* in a pot of boiling salted water. Add the green peas to the pot about 3 minutes before the pasta is done cooking. Drain.

2. In the same pot, mix the cream with the mustard, ham and onion. Season with salt and pepper. Bring to a boil and simmer over medium-low heat for 3 to 4 minutes.

3. Add the pasta and green peas. Reheat for 1 minute, stirring.

 You can replace the pasta shells with any type of short pasta!

SIDE DISH IDEA

Green Apple Salad

In a salad bowl, mix 60 ml (¼ cup) olive oil with 15 ml (1 tbsp) fresh lemon juice, 15 ml (1 tbsp) whole-grain mustard, 60 ml (¼ cup) chopped fresh parsley and 30 ml (2 tbsp) maple syrup. Season with salt and pepper. Add 4 green apples, cut into thin wedges, and 125 ml (½ cup) chopped walnuts. Toss.

1 **Italian sausages**
450 g (1 lb)

2 **Rigatoni**
750 ml (3 cups)

3 **Marinara sauce**
store-bought
500 ml (2 cups)

4 **Mushrooms**
sliced
1 container (227 g)

5 **Baby spinach**
500 ml (2 cups)

ALSO NEEDED:
● **Olive oil**
30 ml (2 tbsp)

OPTIONAL:
● **Fresh basil**
chopped
45 ml (3 tbsp)

One-Pot Sausage Pasta

Prep time **15 minutes** · Cook time **12 minutes** · Serves **4**

PER SERVING	
Calories	697
Protein	27 g
Fat	37 g
Carbohydrates	65 g
Fibre	9 g
Iron	3 mg
Calcium	76 mg
Sodium	1,155 mg

Preparation

1. Remove the casing from the sausages and break up the meat into pieces.

2. In a pot, place the rigatoni, marinara sauce, mushrooms, spinach, sausage meat, oil, and basil if desired. Pour in 500 ml (2 cups) of water. Season with salt and pepper, and stir. Bring to a boil and cover. Let simmer for 12 to 14 minutes, stirring occasionally, until the pasta is *al dente* and the liquid is completely absorbed.

HOMEMADE VERSION
Marinara Sauce

Heat 15 ml (1 tbsp) olive oil in a pot over medium heat. Cook 1 chopped onion and 15 ml (1 tbsp) minced garlic for 1 minute. Add 1 can (540 ml) diced tomatoes and 250 ml (1 cup) strained tomatoes. Season with salt and pepper. Bring to a boil and let simmer over medium-low heat for 10 to 12 minutes.

Pesto Penne

Prep time **15 minutes** · Cook time **12 minutes** · Serves **4**

PER SERVING	
Calories	622
Protein	26 g
Fat	27 g
Carbohydrates	71 g
Fibre	9 g
Iron	3 mg
Calcium	282 mg
Sodium	386 mg

Preparation

1. Cook the pasta *al dente* in a pot of boiling salted water. Drain.

2. Heat a little olive oil in the same pot over medium heat. Cook the cherry tomatoes, and olives if desired, for 1 to 2 minutes.

3. Add the pesto, pasta and bocconcini pearls. Season with salt and pepper. Reheat for 1 minute, stirring.

4. Divide the pasta onto plates. Top with Parmesan.

You can replace the basil pesto with any type of pesto!

1 **Penne**
750 ml (3 cups)

2 **15 to 20 cherry tomatoes**
cut in half

3 **Basil pesto**
store-bought
60 ml (¼ cup)

4 **Bocconcini pearls**
1 container (200 g)

5 **Parmesan**
grated or shaved
80 ml (⅓ cup)

OPTIONAL:
● **16 Kalamata olives**
pitted

HOMEMADE VERSION
Basil Pesto

In a bowl, place 250 ml (1 cup) firmly packed, fresh basil leaves, 1 minced clove of garlic, 80 ml (⅓ cup) grated Parmesan, 125 ml (½ cup) olive oil and 45 ml (3 tbsp) pine nuts. Season with salt and pepper. Use an immersion blender to blend the pesto until it reaches the desired consistency.

1 **Spaghetti**
350 g (about ¾ lb)

2 **Frozen diced vegetable mix**
500 ml (2 cups)

3 **Italian seasoning**
15 ml (1 tbsp)

4 **Marinara sauce**
625 ml (2½ cups)

5 **Brown lentils**
rinsed and drained
1 can (398 ml)

Lentil Spaghetti

Prep time **15 minutes** · Cook time **22 minutes** · Serves **4**

Preparation

1. Cook the pasta *al dente* in a pot of boiling salted water. Drain.

2. Heat a little olive oil in the same pot over medium heat. Cook the vegetable mix for 2 to 3 minutes.

3. Add the Italian seasoning, marinara sauce and lentils. Season with salt and pepper, and stir. Bring to a boil and let simmer over low heat for 10 to 12 minutes.

4. Add the pasta and stir.

 Check out our recipe for homemade frozen diced vegetable mix on page 25.

PER SERVING	
Calories	550
Protein	20 g
Fat	10 g
Carbohydrates	94 g
Fibre	12 g
Iron	4 mg
Calcium	130 mg
Sodium	614 mg

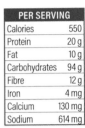

A LITTLE EXTRA

Eggplant Parmesan Croutons

Peel 1 small eggplant and cut it into small cubes. Set out three shallow bowls. Pour 125 ml (½ cup) flour into the first. Beat 2 eggs in the second. In the third, mix 180 ml (¾ cup) panko breadcrumbs with 125 ml (½ cup) grated Parmesan and 15 ml (1 tbsp) chopped fresh thyme. Coat the eggplant cubes in flour, dip them into the beaten eggs and coat them with the breadcrumb mixture. Shake to remove any excess breadcrumbs. Heat 60 ml (¼ cup) olive oil in a frying pan over medium heat. Cook a few eggplant cubes at a time for 4 to 5 minutes. Drain on paper towels. Season with salt and pepper.

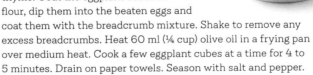

Salmon Lasagna

Prep time **15 minutes** · Cook time **40 minutes** · Serves **4**

PER SERVING	
Calories	905
Protein	66 g
Fat	51 g
Carbohydrates	81 g
Fibre	4 g
Iron	4 mg
Calcium	395 mg
Sodium	1,642 mg

Preparation

1. Preheat the oven to 205°C (400°F).

2. Cook the pasta *al dente* in a pot of boiling salted water. Drain.

3. Bring the Alfredo sauce to a boil in the same pot.

4. Add the salmon, spinach, and dill if desired. Bring to a boil again, stirring occasionally. Season with salt and pepper.

5. Spread a bit of the salmon sauce in the bottom of a 33 cm x 23 cm (13 in x 9 in) baking dish. Cover with 4 lasagna sheets and top with a third of the remaining salmon sauce. Repeat these steps for two more layers. Cover with the remaining lasagna sheets. Top with mozzarella. Bake for 30 to 35 minutes.

⇨ Check out our recipe for homemade Alfredo sauce on page 56.

1 **16 lasagna sheets**

2 **Roasted garlic Alfredo sauce**
750 ml (3 cups)

3 **Salmon**
675 g (about 1½ lb)
skinless fillet, cut
into small cubes

4 **Baby spinach**
1 container (142 g)

5 **Mozzarella**
shredded
500 ml (2 cups)

OPTIONAL:
● **Fresh dill**
chopped
30 ml (2 tbsp)

SIDE DISH IDEA

Leek Salad

Cook 2 leeks, sliced, in a pot of boiling salted water for 1 minute. Rinse under cold water and drain. In a salad bowl, mix 60 ml (¼ cup) olive oil with 30 ml (2 tbsp) balsamic vinegar, 15 ml (1 tbsp) whole-grain mustard, 30 ml (2 tbsp) chopped fresh basil and 10 ml (2 tsp) minced garlic. Season with salt and pepper. Add the leeks, 1 cubed red pepper and 1 cubed yellow pepper. Stir.

1 **Large pasta shells**
750 ml (3 cups)

2 **Medium
ground beef**
450 g (1 lb)

3 **Taco seasoning**
store-bought
1 packet (24 g)

4 **3 pepper halves**
various colours
chopped

5 **Mild salsa**
500 ml (2 cups)

OPTIONAL:
● **Green onions**
chopped
30 ml (2 tbsp)

Taco Pasta

Prep time **15 minutes** · Cook time **19 minutes** · Serves **4**

PER SERVING	
Calories	599
Protein	31 g
Fat	22 g
Carbohydrates	65 g
Fibre	6 g
Iron	6 mg
Calcium	81 mg
Sodium	1,210 mg

Preparation

1. Cook the pasta *al dente* in a pot of boiling salted water. Drain.

2. Heat a little olive oil in the same pot over medium heat. Cook the ground beef for 5 to 7 minutes, breaking up the meat with a wooden spoon, until it is no longer pink.

3. Add the taco seasoning, peppers and salsa. Stir.
Cook for 4 to 5 minutes.

4. Add the pasta and stir.

5. Divide the pasta onto plates. Garnish with green onions if desired.

HOMEMADE VERSION

Taco Seasoning

Combine 2.5 ml (½ tsp) cumin with 20 ml (4 tsp) chili powder, 2.5 ml (½ tsp) ground coriander and 2.5 ml (½ tsp) onion powder.

1 **Macaroni**
750 ml (3 cups)

2 **1 head broccoli**
cut into small florets

3 **Butter**
80 ml (⅓ cup)

4 **2% milk**
625 ml (2½ cups)

5 **Sharp yellow Cheddar**
shredded
300 g (⅔ lb)

ALSO NEEDED:
● **Flour**
80 ml (⅓ cup)

Broccoli Mac and Cheese

Prep time **15 minutes** · Cook time **12 minutes** · Serves **4**

PER SERVING	
Calories	868
Protein	35 g
Fat	48 g
Carbohydrates	81 g
Fibre	3 g
Iron	2 mg
Calcium	633 mg
Sodium	707 mg

Preparation

1. Cook the pasta *al dente* in a pot of boiling salted water. Add the broccoli to the pot about 3 minutes before the pasta is done cooking. Drain.

2. Melt the butter in the same pot over medium heat. Sprinkle in the flour and stir. Cook for 30 seconds, without letting the flour brown.

3. Pour in the milk and bring to a boil, whisking.

4. Add the Cheddar and stir until melted.

5. Add the pasta and broccoli. Season with salt and pepper, and stir. Reheat for 1 minute, stirring.

A LITTLE EXTRA

Bacon and Shallot Topping

Heat a frying pan over medium heat. Cook 8 chopped slices of bacon for 6 to 7 minutes, until crispy. Drain on paper towels. Remove excess fat from the pan. In the same pan, cook 4 sliced shallots over medium-low heat for 2 to 3 minutes. Put bacon back in the pan and stir.

1 Orzo
375 ml (1½ cups)

2 Assorted mushrooms
sliced
1 package (227 g)

3 Cooking cream (15%)
375 ml (1½ cups)

4 Parmesan
grated
180 ml (¾ cup)

5 Baby spinach
1 container (142 g)

ALSO NEEDED:
• **1 onion**
chopped

Creamy Spinach and Mushroom Orzo

Prep time **15 minutes** · Cook time **17 minutes** · Serves **4**

PER SERVING	
Calories	541
Protein	20 g
Fat	25 g
Carbohydrates	60 g
Fibre	4 g
Iron	3 mg
Calcium	384 mg
Sodium	385 mg

Preparation

1. Cook the pasta *al dente* in a pot of boiling salted water. Drain.

2. Heat a little olive oil in the same pot over medium heat. Cook the mushrooms for 3 to 4 minutes.

3. Add the onion and stir. Cook for 1 minute.

4. Add the cream and Parmesan. Season with salt and pepper, and stir. Bring to a boil and simmer over medium-low heat for 3 to 4 minutes.

5. Add the pasta and spinach. Reheat for 1 minute, stirring.

 You can replace the orzo with any type of short pasta!

A LITTLE EXTRA
Roasted Almond Topping

Melt 30 ml (2 tbsp) butter in a frying pan over medium heat. Add 250 ml (1 cup) whole almonds, 30 ml (2 tbsp) maple syrup, 10 ml (2 tsp) smoked sweet paprika and 5 ml (1 tsp) chopped fresh tarragon. Cook for 1 to 2 minutes, stirring.

1 **Penne**
750 ml (3 cups)

2 **Chicken**
3 skinless breasts
cut into small cubes

3 **1 small red onion**
chopped

4 **Roasted red
peppers**
store-bought
chopped
250 ml (1 cup)

5 **Cooking cream
(15%)**
250 ml (1 cup)

OPTIONAL:
● **Fresh basil**
chopped
60 ml (¼ cup)

Chicken Penne with Roasted Pepper Sauce

Prep time **15 minutes** · Cook time **18 minutes** · Serves **4**

PER SERVING	
Calories	618
Protein	34 g
Fat	21 g
Carbohydrates	73 g
Fibre	3 g
Iron	3 mg
Calcium	67 mg
Sodium	265 mg

Preparation

1. Cook the pasta *al dente* in a pot of boiling salted water. Drain.

2. Heat a little olive oil in the same pot over medium heat. Cook the chicken cubes for 4 to 5 minutes, until cooked through. Transfer the chicken to a plate.

3. Heat a little olive oil in the same pot over medium heat. Cook the onion for 1 minute.

4. Add the roasted peppers and cream. Stir. Bring to a boil and simmer over medium-low heat for 3 to 4 minutes.

5. Use an immersion blender to blend the roasted pepper mixture until creamy.

6. Add the pasta, chicken, and basil if desired to the pot. Season with salt and pepper. Reheat for 1 minute, stirring.

HOMEMADE VERSION
Roasted Peppers

Cut 3 red peppers in half. Remove the white membranes and seeds. Place the pepper halves on a baking sheet lined with parchment paper, cut side down. Bake for 20 to 25 minutes at 205°C (400°F). Transfer the peppers to an airtight bag. Seal the bag and let sit for 10 minutes. Gently remove the skin from the peppers and cut them into strips. Sprinkle the pepper strips with 15 ml (1 tbsp) salad seasoning and drizzle them with 15 ml (1 tbsp) olive oil.

1 **Linguine**
350 g (about ¾ lb)

2 **1 leek**
chopped

3 **Bacon**
8 slices, chopped

4 **Mushrooms**
chopped
1 container (227 g)

5 **Parmesan**
grated
125 ml (½ cup)

ALSO NEEDED:
• **Garlic**
2 cloves, minced

OPTIONAL:
• **Fresh parsley**
chopped
60 ml (¼ cup)

Leek and Bacon Linguine

Prep time **15 minutes** · Cook time **16 minutes** · Serves **4**

PER SERVING	
Calories	644
Protein	26 g
Fat	28 g
Carbohydrates	72 g
Fibre	5 g
Iron	5 mg
Calcium	188 mg
Sodium	633 mg

Preparation

1. Cook the pasta *al dente* in a pot of boiling salted water. Add the leek to the pot about 5 minutes before the pasta is done cooking. Drain.

2. Cook the bacon for 3 to 4 minutes in the same pot over medium heat.

3. Add the mushrooms and garlic. Stir. Cook for 2 minutes until the bacon is golden brown.

4. Add the pasta, Parmesan, and parsley if desired. Drizzle with olive oil. Season with salt and pepper. Reheat for 1 minute, stirring.

SIDE DISH IDEA

Four-Cheese Pull-Apart Bread

Slice a grid pattern into 1 round loaf of bread, without cutting all the way through. In a bowl, mix 375 ml (1½ cups) Italian shredded cheese blend with 15 ml (1 tbsp) Italian seasoning and 60 ml (¼ cup) melted butter. Carefully distribute the cheese mixture, spreading it as deep into the slits in the loaf as possible. Place the loaf on a baking sheet lined with parchment paper. Bake for 20 to 25 minutes at 190°C (375°F).

1 **Cheese tortellini**
1 package (350 g)

2 **1 onion**
chopped

3 **Garlic tomato sauce**
375 ml (1½ cups)

4 **Cooking cream (15%)**
125 ml (½ cup)

5 **Parmesan**
grated or shaved
80 ml (⅓ cup)

Tortellini in Rosée Sauce

Prep time **15 minutes** · Cook time **14 minutes** · Serves **4**

PER SERVING	
Calories	445
Protein	18 g
Fat	17 g
Carbohydrates	55 g
Fibre	4 g
Iron	2 mg
Calcium	297 mg
Sodium	1,097 mg

Preparation

1. Cook the pasta *al dente* in a pot of boiling salted water. Drain.

2. Heat a little olive oil in the same pot over medium heat. Cook the onion for 1 minute.

3. Add the tomato sauce and cream. Stir. Bring to a boil and let simmer for 3 minutes.

4. Add the tortellini and Parmesan. Season with salt and pepper. Reheat for 1 minute, stirring.

 You can replace the cheese tortellini with any type of tortellini or ravioli!

SIDE DISH IDEA

Spinach and Mushroom Salad with Croutons

In a salad bowl, mix 60 ml (¼ cup) olive oil with 30 ml (2 tbsp) fresh lemon juice and 15 ml (1 tbsp) whole-grain mustard. Season with salt and pepper. Add 1 container (142 g) baby spinach, 1 red onion, chopped, 8 mushrooms, sliced, and 375 ml (1½ cups) seasoned salad croutons. Toss.

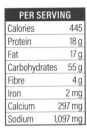

1 **Capellini**
350 g (about ¾ lb)

2 **Butter**
60 ml (¼ cup)

3 **24 medium
shrimp
(31–40 per pound)**
raw and peeled

4 **Fresh parsley**
chopped
60 ml (¼ cup)

5 **1 lemon**
juice and zest

ALSO NEEDED:
● **Garlic**
   chopped
   15 ml (1 tbsp)

OPTIONAL:
● **Pepper flakes**
   1.25 ml (¼ tsp)

Lemon Shrimp Capellini

Prep time **15 minutes** · Cook time **14 minutes** · Serves **4**

PER SERVING	
Calories	484
Protein	23 g
Fat	13 g
Carbohydrates	67 g
Fibre	3 g
Iron	2 mg
Calcium	74 mg
Sodium	502 mg

Preparation

1. Cook the pasta *al dente* in a pot of boiling salted water. Drain.

2. Melt the butter in the same pot over medium heat. Cook the shrimp for 1 to 2 minutes on each side.

3. Add the garlic, parsley and lemon zest and juice. Season with salt. Add the pepper flakes if desired. Cook for 1 minute, stirring.

4. Add the capellini. Reheat for 1 minute, stirring.

 You can replace the capellini with any type of long pasta!

SIDE DISH IDEA

Parmesan Croutons

Cut ⅓ baguette into 12 slices. Place the slices on a baking sheet lined with parchment paper. Top the slices with 250 ml (1 cup) grated Parmesan. Sprinkle with 15 ml (1 tbsp) chopped fresh thyme. Bake for 10 to 12 minutes at 180°C (350°F).

1 **8 lasagna sheets**

2 **Medium ground beef**
450 g (1 lb)

3 **Frozen diced vegetable mix**
500 ml (2 cups)

4 **Tomato sauce with herbs**
625 ml (2½ cups)

5 **Parmesan**
grated
375 ml (1½ cups)

Deconstructed Skillet Lasagna

Prep time **15 minutes** · Cook time **28 minutes** · Serves **4**

PER SERVING	
Calories	722
Protein	46 g
Fat	33 g
Carbohydrates	55 g
Fibre	5 g
Iron	5 mg
Calcium	556 mg
Sodium	1,403 mg

Preparation

1. Cook the pasta *al dente* in a pot of boiling salted water. Drain.

2. Heat a little olive oil in a large skillet over medium heat. Cook the ground beef for 5 to 7 minutes, breaking up the meat with a wooden spoon, until it is no longer pink.

3. Add the vegetable mix and stir. Cook for 2 minutes.

4. Add the tomato sauce. Season with salt and pepper, and stir. Bring to a boil and let simmer over low heat for 10 to 12 minutes.

5. Cut the lasagna sheets into large pieces and add them to the skillet. Reheat for 1 minute, stirring.

6. Cover with Parmesan and let it melt for a few seconds.

⇨ Check out our recipe for homemade frozen diced vegetable mix on page 25.

A LITTLE EXTRA
Savoury Ricotta Cream

Mix 250 ml (1 cup) ricotta cheese with 30 ml (2 tbsp) chopped fresh chives, 15 ml (1 tbsp) lemon zest and 15 ml (1 tbsp) chopped fresh parsley. Season with salt and pepper.

1 Farfalle
750 ml (3 cups)

2 Asparagus
cut into pieces
300 g (⅔ lb)

3 2% milk
250 ml (1 cup)

4 Herb and garlic
cream cheese
1 container (340 g)

5 Smoked salmon
cut into pieces
2 packages
(120 g each)

ALSO NEEDED:
- **1 small red onion**
  diced

OPTIONAL:
- **Fresh dill**
  chopped
  15 ml (1 tbsp)

Smoked Salmon and Asparagus Farfalle

Prep time **15 minutes** · Cook time **11 minutes** · Serves **4**

PER SERVING	
Calories	616
Protein	35 g
Fat	31 g
Carbohydrates	50 g
Fibre	4 g
Iron	4 mg
Calcium	132 mg
Sodium	817 mg

Preparation

1. Cook the pasta *al dente* in a pot of boiling salted water. Add the asparagus to the pot about 3 minutes before the pasta is done cooking. Drain.

2. Add the milk and cream cheese to the same pot and bring to a boil. Stir until smooth.

3. Add the smoked salmon, onion, pasta, asparagus, and dill if desired. Season with salt and pepper. Reheat for 1 minute, stirring.

 You can replace the garlic and herb cream cheese with any flavoured cream cheese! Try plain, vegetable, or chive and onion!

SIDE DISH IDEA

Pancetta, Strawberry and Arugula Salad

Heat a frying pan over medium heat. Brown 250 ml (1 cup) cooked, diced pancetta for 2 to 3 minutes. Remove from heat and let cool. In a salad bowl, mix 125 ml (½ cup) plain yogurt with 15 ml (1 tbsp) whole-grain mustard, 30 ml (2 tbsp) olive oil and 30 ml (2 tbsp) chopped fresh chives. Season with salt and pepper. Add 1 package (142 g) of arugula, 6 strawberries, cut in half, and the pancetta to the salad bowl. Toss.

1 Macaroni
750 ml (3 cups)

2 Frozen diced
vegetable mix
500 ml (2 cups)

3 Condensed cream
of chicken soup
1 can (284 ml)

4 Tuna
drained
3 cans (170 g each)

5 Seasoned salad
croutons
lightly crushed
500 ml (2 cups)

ALSO NEEDED:
● **2% milk**
250 ml (1 cup)

OPTIONAL:
● **Fresh basil**
chopped
45 ml (3 tbsp)

Tuna Macaroni Casserole

Prep time **15 minutes** · Cook time **30 minutes** · Serves **4**

PER SERVING	
Calories	707
Protein	43 g
Fat	17 g
Carbohydrates	96 g
Fibre	5 g
Iron	3 mg
Calcium	140 mg
Sodium	964 mg

Preparation

1. Preheat the oven to 205°C (400°F).

2. Cook the pasta *al dente* in a pot of boiling salted water. Drain.

3. Heat a little olive oil in the same pot over medium heat. Cook the vegetable mix for 2 to 3 minutes.

4. Add the cream of chicken soup and milk. Season with salt and pepper, and stir. Bring to a boil and simmer over medium-low heat for 3 to 4 minutes.

5. Add the pasta, tuna, and basil if desired. Stir.

6. Pour the mixture into a 23 cm (9 in) baking dish. Top with crushed croutons. Bake for 15 to 18 minutes.

⇨ Check out our recipe for homemade cream of chicken soup on page 30.

SIDE DISH IDEA

Colourful Salad

In a salad bowl, mix 500 ml (2 cups) red cabbage, finely chopped, with 2 carrots and half of an English cucumber, cut into thin julienne strips. Add 125 ml (½ cup) Italian vinaigrette and toss.

PIZZAS, BURGERS & MORE

Here's where things get decadent! The following pages are overflowing with dishes to satisfy your every craving in unique and delicious ways. Want proof? Try our famous pizza grilled cheese, our seafood pizza or our barbecue chicken quesadillas!

1 **Pizza dough**
450 g (1 lb)

2 **Basil pesto**
125 ml (½ cup)

3 **3 tomatoes**
sliced

4 **Prosciutto**
10 slices

5 **Italian shredded
cheese blend**
500 ml (2 cups)

Pesto and Prosciutto Pizza

Prep time **15 minutes** • Cook time **20 minutes** • Serves **4**

PER SERVING	
Calories	695
Protein	33 g
Fat	37 g
Carbohydrates	54 g
Fibre	1 g
Iron	4 mg
Calcium	367 mg
Sodium	1,287 mg

Preparation

1. Preheat the oven to 205°C (400°F).

2. On a floured surface, stretch out the pizza dough into a circle, 30 cm (12 in.) in diameter. Place the dough on a baking sheet lined with parchment paper.

3. Brush the dough with pesto. Top with tomato slices and prosciutto. Cover with cheese.

4. Bake for 20 to 25 minutes.

⇨ Check out our recipe for homemade basil pesto on page 248!

SIDE DISH IDEA

Creamy Brussels Sprouts Salad

Use a mandoline to cut 450 g (1 lb) Brussels sprouts into thin slices. In a salad bowl, mix 125 ml (½ cup) plain Greek yogurt with 60 ml (¼ cup) mayonnaise, 15 ml (1 tbsp) onion powder, 30 ml (2 tbsp) maple syrup, 15 ml (1 tbsp) Dijon mustard, 30 ml (2 tbsp) fresh lemon juice and 60 ml (¼ cup) chopped fresh parsley. Add the Brussels sprouts. Season with salt and pepper, and stir.

1 Salmon
4 fillets, 150 g
(⅓ lb) each, skin
removed

2 Cajun spices
15 ml (1 tbsp)

3 1 red pepper
cut into rings

4 4 hamburger buns

**5 Green curly leaf
lettuce**
4 leaves

ALSO NEEDED:
● **1 small red onion**
    cut into thin rounds

Cajun Salmon Burgers

Prep time **15 minutes** • Cook time **8 minutes** • Serves **4**

Preparation

1. Season the salmon fillets with the Cajun spices.

2. Heat a little olive oil in a frying pan over medium heat. Cook the salmon fillets for 3 to 4 minutes on each side. Set the salmon aside on a plate.

3. In the same pan, cook the pepper for 1 to 2 minutes.

4. Heat another frying pan over medium-low heat. Slice the buns in half and toast them in the pan for 30 seconds on each side.

5. Fill each bun with a lettuce leaf, a salmon fillet, pepper and red onion.

⇨   Check out our recipe for homemade Cajun spice mix on page 104!

PER SERVING	
Calories	509
Protein	36 g
Fat	26 g
Carbohydrates	30 g
Fibre	2 g
Iron	2 mg
Calcium	50 mg
Sodium	389 mg

A LITTLE EXTRA

Avocado Sauce

In a bowl, mix 1 avocado, 30 ml (2 tbsp) sour cream, 15 ml (1 tbsp) lime zest and 30 ml (2 tbsp) fresh cilantro leaves. Season with salt and pepper. Use an immersion blender to mix until smooth.

280

1 **Rye bread**
8 slices

2 **Dijon mustard**
80 ml (⅓ cup)

3 **Smoked meat**
sliced
450 g (1 lb)

4 **Swiss cheese**
8 slices

5 **Butter**
45 ml (3 tbsp)

Smoked Meat Grilled Cheese

Prep time **15 minutes** • Cook time **4 minutes** • Serves **4**

PER SERVING	
Calories	549
Protein	41 g
Fat	28 g
Carbohydrates	31 g
Fibre	3 g
Iron	4 mg
Calcium	178 mg
Sodium	1,446 mg

Preparation

1. Spread each slice of bread with mustard.

2. Top four slices of bread with smoked meat and slices of Swiss cheese. Cover with the four remaining slices of bread.

3. Melt the butter in a frying pan over medium-low heat. Cook the grilled cheese sandwiches for 2 minutes on each side, until the cheese is melted.

 You can replace the Swiss cheese with Cheddar, mozzarella or provolone!

SIDE DISH IDEA

Potato Salad with Pickles

Peel 5 large potatoes and cut them into cubes. Place the cubed potatoes in a pot and cover with cold water. Season with salt. Bring to a boil and cook for 18 to 20 minutes, until the potatoes are cooked but still slightly crunchy. Drain and rinse with cold water. In a salad bowl, mix 125 ml (½ cup) mayonnaise with 125 ml (½ cup) plain Greek yogurt, 15 ml (1 tbsp) Dijon mustard, 4 chopped green onions, 60 ml (¼ cup) chopped fresh parsley and 125 ml (½ cup) chopped baby dill pickles. Add the potatoes. Season with salt and pepper, and stir.

1 **Whole tomatoes**
drained
1 can (796 ml)

2 **Garlic**
chopped
15 ml (1 tbsp)

3 **4 naan breads**

4 **Fresh mozzarella**
sliced
450 g (1 lb)

5 **Fresh basil**
125 ml (½ cup)
leaves

ALSO NEEDED:
● **1 small red onion**
chopped

Margherita Naan Pizzas

Prep time **15 minutes** • Cook time **15 minutes** • Serves **4**

PER SERVING	
Calories	598
Protein	24 g
Fat	33 g
Carbohydrates	56 g
Fibre	1 g
Iron	4 mg
Calcium	720 mg
Sodium	1,150 mg

Preparation

1. Preheat the oven to 205°C (400°F).

2. Place the tomatoes in a bowl and crush them lightly with a fork. Add the garlic and stir.

3. Place the naan breads on two baking sheets lined with parchment paper. Spread with the crushed tomatoes and top with fresh mozzarella and onion. Season with salt and pepper.

4. Bake for 15 to 18 minutes.

5. Remove the pizzas from the oven and garnish with basil.

 You can replace the naan breads with tortillas, pita bread or any other kind of flatbread!

┌─ **A LITTLE EXTRA**
Herbed Oil

Mix 60 ml (¼ cup) olive oil with 1.25 ml (¼ tsp) red pepper flakes, 15 ml (1 tbsp) lemon zest and 15 ml (1 tbsp) chopped fresh oregano. Season with salt.

284

1 **Haloumi**
(grilling cheese)
cut into 4 slices
300 g (⅔ lb)

2 **4 hamburger buns**

3 **Hummus**
250 ml (1 cup)

4 **Romaine lettuce**
4 leaves

5 **Roasted red peppers**
250 ml (1 cup)

ALSO NEEDED:
● **1 small red onion**
cut into 4 rounds

Haloumi Burgers

Prep time **15 minutes** • Cook time **5 minutes** • Serves **4**

PER SERVING	
Calories	596
Protein	24 g
Fat	38 g
Carbohydrates	43 g
Fibre	6 g
Iron	2 mg
Calcium	778 mg
Sodium	1,517 mg

Preparation

1. Heat a non-stick pan over medium heat and cook the haloumi slices for 1 minute on each side. Remove from the pan and set aside on a plate.

2. Heat a little olive oil in the same frying pan over medium heat. Cook the onion rounds for 1 minute on each side.

3. Heat another frying pan over medium-low heat. Slice the buns in half and toast them in the pan for 30 seconds on each side.

4. Spread the buns with hummus. Top with lettuce, roasted peppers, haloumi and onion.

⇨ Check out our recipe for homemade roasted red peppers on page 260!

SIDE DISH IDEA

Roasted Sweet Potatoes

Cut 4 sweet potatoes into quarters. In a bowl, mix the sweet potatoes with 15 ml (1 tbsp) olive oil, 15 ml (1 tbsp) Cajun spices and 15 ml (1 tbsp) smoked sweet paprika. Season with salt and pepper, and stir. Spread the sweet potatoes on a baking sheet lined with parchment paper. Bake for 20 to 25 minutes at 205°C (400°F), turning the sweet potatoes at the halfway point.

1 **Barbecue sauce**
180 ml (¾ cup)

2 **Chicken**
cooked and sliced
500 ml (2 cups)

3 **Fresh cilantro**
chopped
30 ml (2 tbsp)

4 **8 small tortillas**

5 **Tex-Mex shredded cheese**
500 ml (2 cups)

ALSO NEEDED:
● **1 small red onion**
chopped

OPTIONAL:
● **Sour cream (14%)**
125 ml (½ cup)

Barbecue Chicken Quesadillas

Prep time **15 minutes** • Cook time **4 minutes** • Serves **4**

PER SERVING	
Calories	666
Protein	43 g
Fat	28 g
Carbohydrates	58 g
Fibre	2 g
Iron	4 mg
Calcium	140 mg
Sodium	1,112 mg

Preparation

1. In a bowl, mix the barbecue sauce with the cooked chicken, onion and cilantro.

2. Spread a quarter of the prepared chicken over half of each tortilla. Top with cheese. Fold the other half of the tortillas over the filling.

3. Heat a little olive oil in a frying pan over low heat. Cook the quesadillas for 2 to 3 minutes on each side.

4. Serve the quesadillas with sour cream if desired.

SIDE DISH IDEA

Avocado Salad

In a salad bowl, mix 80 ml (⅓ cup) mayonnaise with 60 ml (¼ cup) plain Greek yogurt, 15 ml (1 tbsp) lime zest, 30 ml (2 tbsp) fresh lime juice, 1.25 ml (¼ tsp) chipotle powder and 30 ml (2 tbsp) chopped fresh parsley. Add 3 avocados, cut into cubes. Season with salt and pepper, and stir gently.

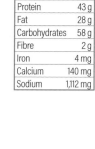

1 **Lean ground beef**
450 g (1 lb)

2 **HP sauce**
store-bought
80 ml (⅓ cup)

3 **Pizza dough**
450 g (1 lb)

4 **2 green peppers**
sliced

5 **Mozzarella**
shredded
500 ml (2 cups)

ALSO NEEDED:
● **2 onions**
chopped

Philly Cheesesteak Pizza

Prep time **15 minutes** • Cook time **22 minutes** • Serves **4**

PER SERVING	
Calories	802
Protein	45 g
Fat	39 g
Carbohydrates	65 g
Fibre	2 g
Iron	6 mg
Calcium	377 mg
Sodium	1,164 mg

Preparation

1. Preheat the oven to 205°C (400°F).

2. Heat a little olive oil in a frying pan over medium heat. Cook the ground beef for 5 to 7 minutes, breaking up the meat with a wooden spoon, until it is no longer pink.

3. Add the onions and cook for 1 minute.

4. Add the HP sauce. Season with salt and pepper, and stir. Cook for 1 to 2 minutes.

5. On a floured surface, stretch out the pizza dough into a circle, 30 cm (12 in.) in diameter. Place the dough on a baking sheet lined with parchment paper.

6. Top the pizza with the ground beef, green onions and mozzarella.

7. Bake for 20 to 25 minutes.

HOMEMADE VERSION
HP-Style Steak Sauce

Bring 180 ml (¾ cup) water to boil in a pot. Add 125 ml (½ cup) pitted dates, 90 ml (⅓ cup + 2 tsp) cider vinegar, 30 ml (2 tbsp) molasses and 30 ml (2 tbsp) tomato paste. Season with salt. Bring to a boil, stirring constantly. Use an immersion blender to mix until smooth. If the sauce is too thick, add a little water. Continue cooking for 2 minutes over low heat.

1 **4 mild Italian sausages**

2 **1 baguette**

3 **Mayonnaise** 80 ml (⅓ cup)

4 **Dijon mustard** 60 ml (¼ cup)

5 **Coleslaw vegetable mix** 375 ml (1½ cups)

European Hot-Dog

Prep time **15 minutes** • Cook time **10 minutes** • Serves **4**

Preparation

1. Heat a little olive oil in a frying pan over medium heat. Cook the sausages for 10 to 12 minutes, until they are no longer pink inside.

2. Cut the baguette into four pieces. Slice each piece open, without cutting all the way through.

3. Fill each bun with mayonnaise, mustard and a sausage, and top with coleslaw mix.

💡 You can replace the Italian sausages with any other kind of sausage you prefer!

PER SERVING	
Calories	520
Protein	17 g
Fat	31 g
Carbohydrates	41 g
Fibre	4 g
Iron	2 mg
Calcium	32 mg
Sodium	1,368 mg

SIDE DISH IDEA

Veggie Chips

Use a mandoline to cut 2 potatoes and 2 sweet potatoes into thin slices. Rinse the slices thoroughly in cold water. Drain, then dry on a dish towel. Slice 2 carrots into thin ribbons. Heat 2 l (8 cups) canola oil in a deep fryer or a large pot until it reaches 163°C (325°F) on a cooking thermometer. If you are using a pot, make sure the oil doesn't overheat and catch fire. Fry a few vegetable slices at a time for 2 to 3 minutes, until golden and crunchy. Drain the chips on paper towel. Season with salt and pepper.

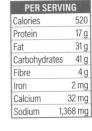

1 Chicken
3 skinless breasts

2 Chili powder
15 ml (1 tbsp)

3 Tortilla chips
1 bag (275 g)

4 Corn kernels
250 ml (1 cup)

**5 Tex-Mex shredded
cheese**
375 ml (1½ cups)

OPTIONAL:
● **Black olives**
sliced
180 ml (¾ cup)

Chicken Nachos

Prep time **15 minutes** • Cook time **30 minutes** • Serves **4**

PER SERVING	
Calories	687
Protein	37 g
Fat	36 g
Carbohydrates	56 g
Fibre	6 g
Iron	2 mg
Calcium	94 mg
Sodium	1,052 mg

Preparation

1. Preheat the oven to 180°C (350°F).

2. Season the chicken breasts with the chili powder.

3. Heat a little olive oil in a frying pan over medium heat. Cook the chicken breasts for 15 to 18 minutes, turning several times, until the meat is no longer pink in the centre. Remove from heat and let cool. Cut the chicken breasts into small pieces.

4. Spread the corn chips over a baking sheet lined with parchment paper. Top with corn, chicken, and olives if desired. Cover with cheese.

5. Bake for 15 to 18 minutes, until the cheese is melted.

 You can also serve these nachos with sour cream and guacamole!

A LITTLE EXTRA

Pico de gallo

Seed and dice 3 Italian tomatoes and mix with 1 small red onion, chopped, 2 jalapeños, seeded and chopped, 30 ml (2 tbsp) fresh lime juice and 45 ml (3 tbsp) chopped fresh cilantro.

1 **Tuna**
drained
3 cans (170 g each)

2 **Ranch dressing**
125 ml (½ cup)

3 **4 sesame seed bagels**

4 **Boston lettuce**
4 leaves

5 **2 Italian tomatoes**
sliced

Tuna Salad Bagels

Prep time **15 minutes** • Serves **4**

Preparation

1. In a bowl, mix the tuna with the ranch dressing.

2. Slice the bagels in half and toast them.

3. Top the bagels with lettuce, tomato, tuna salad and onion.

⇨ Check out our recipe for homemade ranch dressing on page 46.

PER SERVING	
Calories	452
Protein	31 g
Fat	17 g
Carbohydrates	42 g
Fibre	3 g
Iron	5 mg
Calcium	98 mg
Sodium	576 mg

SIDE DISH IDEA

Carrot Salad

In a salad bowl, mix 60 ml (¼ cup) olive oil with 15 ml (1 tbsp) whole-grain mustard, 30 ml (2 tbsp) fresh lemon juice, 15 ml (1 tbsp) honey and 2.5 ml (½ tsp) curry powder. Add 4 carrots, cut into thin julienne strips, and 125 ml (½ cup) golden raisins. Season with salt and pepper, and stir.

ALSO NEEDED:
● **1 small red onion**
cut into thin rounds

1 **Pizza dough**
450 g (1 lb)

2 **Rosée sauce**
500 ml (2 cups)

3 **Pollock**
shredded
300 g (⅔ lb)

4 **Northern shrimp**
150 g (250 ml)

5 **Cheddar**
shredded
500 ml (2 cups)

ALSO NEEDED:
● **1 small red onion**
cut into thin rounds

Seafood Pizza

Prep time **15 minutes** • Cook time **20 minutes** • Serves **4**

PER SERVING	
Calories	790
Protein	37 g
Fat	35 g
Carbohydrates	80 g
Fibre	3 g
Iron	4 mg
Calcium	519 mg
Sodium	1,685 mg

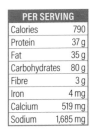

Preparation

1. Preheat the oven to 205°C (400°F).

2. On a floured surface, stretch the pizza dough into a rectangle, 33 cm x 23 cm (13 in x 9 in). Place the dough on a baking sheet lined with parchment paper.

3. Spread the rosée sauce over the dough. Top with pollock, shrimp and onion. Cover with Cheddar.

4. Bake for 20 to 25 minutes.

 You can replace the northern shrimp with any other type of cooked shrimp!

SIDE DISH IDEA

Arugula Salad with Lemon and Parmesan

In a salad bowl, mix 60 ml (¼ cup) olive oil with 30 ml (2 tbsp) fresh lemon juice, 15 ml (1 tbsp) lemon zest, 125 ml (½ cup) grated Parmesan and 45 ml (3 tbsp) chopped fresh chives. Add 1 container (142 g) of arugula. Season with salt and pepper, and stir.

298

1 **Medium ground beef**
450 g (1 lb)

2 **Ketchup**
160 ml (⅔ cup)

3 **Worcestershire sauce**
30 ml (2 tbsp)

4 **Yellow mustard**
30 ml (2 tbsp)

5 **4 hamburger buns**

ALSO NEEDED:
● **1 onion**
   chopped

Sloppy Joes

Prep time **15 minutes** • Cook time **10 minutes** • Serves **4**

Preparation

1. Heat a little olive oil in a frying pan over medium heat. Cook the ground beef for 5 to 7 minutes, breaking up the meat with a wooden spoon, until it is no longer pink.

2. Add the ketchup, Worcestershire sauce, mustard and onion. Season with salt and pepper. Bring to a boil, then let simmer for 6 to 8 minutes over low heat.

3. Heat another frying pan over medium-low heat. Slice the buns in half and toast them in the pan for 30 seconds on each side.

4. Top the buns with the meat mixture.

PER SERVING	
Calories	494
Protein	26 g
Fat	24 g
Carbohydrates	41 g
Fibre	3 g
Iron	4 mg
Calcium	64 mg
Sodium	849 mg

SIDE DISH IDEA

Cucumber Caesar Salad

Use a mandoline to slice 1 English cucumber into thin ribbons. In a salad bowl, mix 125 ml (½ cup) Caesar dressing with 60 ml (¼ cup) cooked bacon, cut into pieces, 45 ml (3 tbsp) chopped fresh parsley and 2 chopped green onions. Add the cucumber and stir.

1 **Multigrain bread**
8 slices

2 **Garlic butter**
store-bought
softened
125 ml (½ cup)

3 **Pizza sauce**
250 ml (1 cup)

4 **Pepperoni**
16 slices

5 **Mozzarella**
shredded
375 ml (1½ cups)

ALSO NEEDED:
● **1 onion**
diced

Pizza Grilled Cheese

Prep time **15 minutes** • Cook time **12 minutes** • Serves **4**

PER SERVING	
Calories	706
Protein	26 g
Fat	49 g
Carbohydrates	45 g
Fibre	6 g
Iron	4 mg
Calcium	397 mg
Sodium	1,714 mg

Preparation

1. Spread one side of each slice of bread with garlic butter.

2. Spread the other side of 4 slices of bread with pizza sauce.
Top with pepperoni, mozzarella and onion.

3. Cover with the remaining slices of bread, buttered side facing up.

4. Heat a non-stick pan over medium heat. Cook the grilled cheese
sandwiches for 3 to 4 minutes on each side, until the cheese is melted.

You can replace the pepperoni with salami, chorizo or any
other cured meats you like!

HOMEMADE VERSION
Garlic Butter

In a bowl, place 125 ml (½ cup)
of softened butter, 10 ml
(2 tsp) minced garlic and
45 ml (3 tbsp) chopped fresh
parsley. Season with salt and
pepper. Use an electric mixer to
whip until smooth and creamy.

Recipe index

Made by

Publisher of